se return or renew by
ɔtest date below

BY PHONE

The New Local Government Series
No. 13

THE LOCAL GOVERNMENT ACT 1972

Problems of Implementation

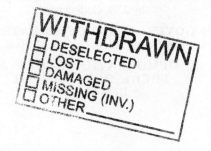

The New Local Government Series

GENERAL EDITOR
PROFESSOR PETER G. RICHARDS

THE LOCAL GOVERNMENT ACT 1972

Problems of Implementation

BY

PETER G. RICHARDS

Professor of British Government
University of Southampton

PEP
12 Upper Belgrave Street, London

London
GEORGE ALLEN & UNWIN LTD
RUSKIN HOUSE   MUSEUM STREET

First published in 1975

Printed in Great Britain
in 10 point Times Linotype
by Willmer Brothers Limited
Birkenhead

PREFACE

This book is the result of a one-man survey of the problems of bringing the Local Government Act 1972 into effect. With the financial assistance of the Social Science Research Council I was released from my normal duties at the University of Southampton during the session 1973–74 and joined Political and Economic Planning.

My work was concentrated on the six metropolitan areas and the English shire counties. Non-metropolitan districts were excluded apart from issues concerning their relationships to the county auth-orities. Wales was excluded altogether. Information was sought from local authorities about their preparations for the changeover and, in particular, about their new patterns of management. The counties responded well and almost without exception. Two-thirds of the metropolitan districts also co-operated. This material was supple-mented by a large number of interviews held throughout the country with senior local officials who embraced a wide span of professional experience. In addition, further information was gathered by cor-respondence and interview with central sources—government departments and agencies, the associations of local authorities, poli-tical parties and trade unions.

The intention is to provide a broad picture of events and to avoid excessive local detail. However, local events have been described where they raise problems of general interest. Inevitably, my treat-ment of local matters is highly selective. One man alone cannot visit all the major departments of all major local authorities. As it is, in a book of this size, much of the local material collected has not been used except as support for more generalised statements. In no sense can this book present a total picture of the reorganisation. There is great scope for further specialised and local studies of the conse-quences of the 1972 Act.

I am grateful to a very large number of people and organisations for their assistance. PEP has provided me with a base and much wise advice and clerical support. It organised an advisory com-mittee whose members have provided information and invaluable comments on the pattern of my work. In particular the Chairman, Dr Hedley Marshall, has been a very great help. I am also grateful to the many officials, local and national, who found time to send me information, answer specific queries by correspondence and in many cases to talk to me personally. To arrange interviews was not always easy. In addition to the inevitable pressures caused by the changeover on 1 April 1974, there were further stresses in the first three months of the year caused by the fuel shortage, the three-day working week and the organisation of a general election. Naturally one wished to talk to representatives of the authorities most severely affected by reorganisation—but at this period of multiple extra burdens it was almost indecent to impose further on their time.

There is some controversial material in the book, so it is unusually necessary to stress that I alone am responsible for the opinions expressed. Finally, it must be emphasised that this is essentially a study of the problems of moving from one administrative structure to another. It is not an assessment of the merits or demerits of the new system. As yet it is too soon for such judgement to be attempted.

Mrs P. E. Dunn typed the early drafts of each chapter. Miss Diana Marshallsay, BA, ALA, has once more taken responsibility for the Index. My wife, as usual, has given meticulous attention to improving the clarity of what I have written.

PETER G. RICHARDS
Red Lodge, Chilworth
November 1974

CONTENTS

Chapter 1

THE NEW PATTERN OF LOCAL AUTHORITIES

Areas

The Local Government Act of 1972 caused a substantial reduction in the number of local authorities. One might expect a reduction to lead to a simplification of the structure. In some areas change did produce a more streamlined system; elsewhere the result was greater complexity. Former county boroughs, which had been all-purpose authorities, were merged into the counties; so the larger towns, which previously had been governed by a single local council, are now administered by separate county and district authorities. Simplification was achieved by the amalgamation of smaller county authorities and a drastic cut in the number of second-tier districts. Small and medium-sized towns which used to rank as non-county boroughs or urban districts within a county lost their separate institutions at second-tier level and were merged with surrounding areas into a new district. Many such towns were allowed to retain a local council with minimal powers at third-tier level: these bodies were given the inglorious name of 'successor parishes'. Overall, the general tendency to have fewer authorities meant that they became larger physically and, it was argued, more remote from the public. The six largest concentrations of population outside London—known as the metropolitan areas—were given a new style of local government which differed from the traditional shires in that education and the social services became a district and not a county responsibility. This change was due to a feeling that a conurbation taken as a whole was too vast to be entrusted with the more personal local government services. Parts of former rural districts on the fringes of these areas were brought within the metropolitan system; here in particular the local inhabitants found themselves transferred into a new style of local administration.

Before the changes were made on 1 April 1974 the structure of English local government outside London took this form:

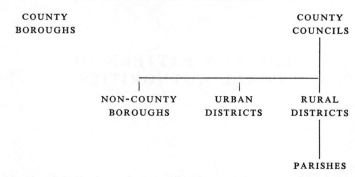

In 1972 there were 79 county boroughs, 45 county councils, 227 non-county boroughs, 449 urban districts and 410 rural districts. Thus there were 1,210 first and second tier local authorities. The new structure is shown below.

Metropolitan areas	Non-metropolitan areas
COUNTIES	COUNTIES
DISTRICTS	DISTRICTS
PARISHES (in former rural areas)[1]	PARISHES (except in larger towns)

It will be seen that the difference in structure—but not in functions —occurs at the third-tier level. There are 6 metropolitan counties containing 36 metropolitan districts, and 39 shire counties[2] containing 296 districts, making a total of 377 first- and second-tier local authorities. This is fractionally more than 30 per cent of the previous figure.

The number of elected councillors was reduced by approximately one-third,[3] a smaller proportionate fall than that in the number of councils. There are two reasons for this variation. In the former county boroughs the total of councillors usually increased because the area is now represented not through a single authority but at county and district levels. Again, in rural areas where district councils were grouped together, the number of councillors although reduced is still high enough to provide a reasonable degree of representation. Thus where four authorities were brought together to form one unit, the probability is that the number of councillors will be between one-half and one-third of the former number—and not one-quarter. The loss of councillors tended to be greatest in areas which previously had formed very small urban authorities: the extreme case before reorganisation was Saxmundham in Suffolk which rejoiced in a ratio of one councillor to 102 electors. The councillor-population ratio still varies from place to place. Generally it is highest in local authorities which have the smallest number of inhabitants, because the Home Office imposed an upper limit of approximately one hundred councillors in each authority. The councillor-population ratio in the average-sized county is around 1 to 12,000 and in the average district around 1 to 2,000. Of course the actual number of people a councillor represents formally may be substantially higher than these figures because in the district councils many wards or electoral divisions return more than one councillor.

A major aim of reorganisation was to reduce disparities in the size of authorities. To some extent this has been achieved. Certainly the variations are less extreme than before the 1972 Act became effective. Even so, sizes are far from uniform. Partly this is due to respect for history and local sentiment; partly it is because conditions do vary in different parts of England. The original intention was that the minimum population for a county should be 250,000. However, at a late stage in the passage of the Bill, the Government agreed that the Isle of Wight should be a separate county and not be joined administratively with Hampshire on the mainland. So the smallest county has little more than 100,000 people. The greater part of the local government map of England still has a close affinity to the traditional shires. This element of continuity was a major political advantage of the 1972 Act as contrasted with the proposals of the Royal Commission. Sporting organisations and other social activities based on the county unit could continue their activities with a minimum of disturbance. From the viewpoint of the new shires the extent of the upheaval depended largely on whether a new authority included former county boroughs. In terms of their composition they can be divided conveniently into seven categories:

A. No change from former county (5);
B. Boundary adjustment to county not containing county borough (6);
C. Unchanged boundary but amalgamation with one or more county boroughs (5);
D. Boundary changes and amalgamation with one or more county boroughs (14);
E. Amalgamation of county councils (1);

F. Amalgamation of county councils and county boroughs (5);
G. Amalgamation of former county boroughs with surrounding hinterland (3).

The categories represent broadly an escalating degree of change. The numbers in brackets show the number of non-metropolitan counties in each group. Some authorities in category B lost territory and others gained, while those in categories C and D gained. For the remaining groups the concepts of loss and gain do not readily apply for here authorities were created on a fresh basis; the same is also essentially true for North Yorkshire in category D for it is markedly different from the former North Riding. Category G involved the greatest change because these three new counties (Avon, Cleveland and Humberside) bear no relation to the traditional shires.

The table on page 15 shows the population of the shire counties, the number of districts and the population range of the districts within each county and the type of change experienced in terms of the categories defined above.

Non-metropolitan districts differ from the counties and the metropolitan districts in that their boundaries were not fixed by the 1972 Act. Instead their boundaries were proposed by the Local Government Boundary Commission for England in its First Report (Cmnd 5148) after a series of local consultations. These proposals were then adopted by the Secretary of State and incorporated in Orders that were submitted for, and obtained, parliamentary approval. In carrying out its task the Boundary Commission had to try and find generally acceptable solutions to local problems. It also had to work within a set of guidelines laid down by the Secretary of State. These covered a variety of factors. The Commission was to aim at a minimum district population of 40,000 while the preferred population range was 75,000–100,000. The identity of large towns and new towns was to be maintained. When considering population levels regard was to be had for local plans for rapid urban expansion. Wherever possible the new districts were to consist of the whole of one or more former authorities and only in special circumstances was bisection of the latter permissible. The Commission was also to take note of the wishes of local inhabitants, the existing pattern of community life, the distribution of parliamentary constituencies and the need, above all, to secure effective operation of local government services.

Three aspects of the guidelines deserve comment. First, the Commission felt obliged to go below the 40,000 population minimum for 14 districts. These are in sparsely populated rural areas where to insist on a population of 40,000 would have increased the geo-

SHIRE COUNTIES: POPULATION AND COMPONENTS

County	Population 1971 (000s)	Number of districts	Population range of districts (000s)	Category of change
Avon	902	6	70–425	G
Bedfordshire	463	4	88–161	C
Berkshire	620	6	63–132	D
Buckinghamshire	476	5	64–141	B
Cambridgeshire	505	6	49–105	E
Cheshire	865	8	70–161	D
Cleveland	567	4	99–163	G
Cornwall	377	6	50– 74	A
Cumbria	476	6	41–100	F
Derbyshire	886	9	61–219	D
Devon	896	10	39–239	C
Dorset	553	8	33–153	D
Durham	608	8	24–108	D
East Sussex	650	7	70–166	D
Essex	1,354	14	40–162	C
Gloucestershire	463	6	62– 90	D
Hampshire	1,370	13	61–214	D
Hereford and Worcester	562	9	33– 84	F
Hertfordshire	922	10	66–121	A
Humberside	838	9	39–285	G
Isle of Wight	109	2	44– 64	A
Kent	1,396	14	78–138	C
Lancashire	1,341	14	51–155	D
Leicestershire	799	9	27–283	F
Lincolnshire	503	7	48– 94	F
Norfolk	624	7	71–121	D
North Yorkshire	629	8	42–128	D
Northamptonshire	468	7	48–133	C
Northumberland	280	6	25– 64	B
Nottinghamshire	973	8	85–299	D
Oxfordshire	504	5	74–133	D
Salop	337	6	30– 97	A
Somerset	387	5	29–114	B
Staffordshire	963	9	40–265	D
Suffolk	537	7	39–122	F
Surrey	981	11	65–118	B
Warwickshire	456	5	58–111	B
West Sussex	610	7	52–105	B
Wiltshire	486	5	64–139	A

graphical size of the districts beyond acceptable limits.[4] Second, the requirement to preserve the identity of large towns cut across a dominant theme in earlier discussions on local government reform— that of the need to integrate towns with their surrounding rural hinterland both in the interest of economic operation of services and to arrange for administrative boundaries to match social realities. A result of this policy is that Bath, Cambridge, Hereford and Scunthorpe are each wholly surrounded by one other district council. Another consequence of not dividing former county boroughs is that some districts are now larger than counties—notably Bristol with a population of 425,000. Third, the pressure to avoid division of existing areas greatly eased the Commission's task. By adhering as firmly as possible to this principle, the Commission minimised the number of alternatives that required consideration. The consequence, admittedly, is not an optimum pattern. But this policy did assist rapid decision-making and helped to reduce local objections. A local council may not welcome amalgamation but it is likely to object even more strongly to dismemberment into separate parts.

There remain many local adjustments which are badly needed and which the Boundary Commission will have to consider in the future, particularly in relation to the boundaries of urban communities which, in many areas, have long been out-of-date due to the rampant march of development. In the event the new boundaries were received with a remarkably high level of acceptance or at least acquiescence. Indeed, the major conflicts on boundaries were aroused not by the actions of the Boundary Commission but by the earlier government decisions on county boundaries which are both more important and far more emotive than district demarcations.[5]

Metropolitan areas have quite a separate set of problems. The top-tier authority in each case was wholly new. In contrast to the shire counties (save those in category G) they had no tradition, premises or staff with which to build a new entity. The second-tier metropolitan districts were formed out of amalgamations of former authorities or parts thereof, ranging in status from county borough to rural district. Only two districts, Liverpool and Wolverhampton, had unchanged boundaries. In a few other cases the changes were trivial: Manchester was enlarged by the addition of the parish of Ringway. A feature of these authorities is that they are not as large as might have been expected. Local opinion was partly responsible. Pressure from the Huyton area of Merseyside and the Bury/Rochdale area of Greater Manchester in each case forced the establishment of an additional district. Some metropolitan districts have a population below 200,000 and so are not as large or as wealthy as the biggest districts outside the metropolitan areas: the comparison is significant because the latter do not administer the expensive education and social welfare services. Another feature of metropolitan districts is that many contain the whole or a part of former rural districts. These areas had third-tier parish institutions under the old structure and this entitlement still remains. Thus while the greater part of metropolitan areas have a two-tier system, the remainder has a third level. The table below summarises the composition of the metropolitan areas.

METROPOLITAN COUNTIES: POPULATION AND COMPOSITION

County	Population 1971 (000s)	Total number of districts	Population range of districts (000s)	Districts containing former rural districts	Largest district
Greater Manchester	2,727	10	174– 522	3	Manchester
Merseyside	1,659	5	192– 607	3	Liverpool
South Yorkshire	1,315	4	226– 566	4	Sheffield
Tyne and Wear	1,209	5	177– 308	3	Newcastle
West Midlands	2,790	7	192–1,096	2	Birmingham
West Yorkshire	2,053	5	194– 738	4	Leeds

Names of all counties were designated in the Act. With one exception these gave little trouble. The Government wished to avoid long clumsy names and, in particular, to avoid the form A and B. The enforced marriage with Worcestershire was deeply resented in Herefordshire and the proposal that the shotgun wedding should be blessed with the name Malvernshire was ill-received. So the Government came to accept the double-barrelled title Hereford and Worcester in order to mollify local opinion. Names for the districts were decided by the Boundary Commission after local consultation. Where a number of authorities had been joined together the most tactful course was often to find a fresh name drawn from a local geographical feature, e.g. a river. Again an attempt was made to avoid clumsy names. Decisions of the Commission were readily accepted in most areas. However, a few authorities invoked Section 74 of the Local Government Act 1972 which allows a local authority to change its name if the proposal is carried by a two-thirds majority at a specially convened meeting of the council. But until 1 April 1978 such a change needs the consent of the Secretary of State.

Some districts enjoy the dignity of being boroughs. The chairmen and vice-chairmen of these councils are entitled to the status of Mayor and Deputy Mayor. To become a borough a district must submit a petition to the Privy Council in accordance with Section 245 of the 1972 Act: the decision to do so must be supported by a two-thirds majority at a special council meeting called for this particular purpose.[6] If the view of the Privy Council is favourable, the district receives a charter which may contain provisions appearing in earlier charters appertaining to former boroughs now included in the district. The practical effect of borough status on the powers of a district is very limited but the social and psychological effects may be considerable. There was conflict in some areas over the desirability of borough status. Representatives from former boroughs often wished to retain the dignities to which they were accustomed while councillors from rural areas objected to the idea of being included in a borough. Elsewhere groups of Labour councillors opposed the quest for borough status. All the 165 applications were successful. In almost every case the new charter represents the continuation of past tradition: a few places, e.g. Fareham, became boroughs for the first time. But the words borough or city no longer apply to distinctively urban areas. The Borough of Restormel and the City of Winchester both spread over hundreds of square miles of open countryside. Every metropolitan district has become a borough with the exception of Sefton. Here there was a strong desire to retain the separate mayoralities of Crosby and Sefton. The device of charter trustees[7] permitted this to be done provided that the Sefton district as a whole was not a borough.

Great ingenuity was devoted to the preservation of the dignities of boroughs that ceased to be principal authorities after reorganisation. Some former boroughs and urban districts were allowed to keep their own separate institutions at third-tier level as 'successor parishes'. Further, the 1972 Act authorised any parish council that does not represent a grouping of parishes to resolve to adopt the title 'town'. Where this has been done the parish council becomes a town council and the chairman is entitled to the style of town mayor. So an ex-borough or ex-urban district area may still survive as a town with a town mayor even if the district of which it is a part has become a borough with the embellishment of its own mayor. The Boundary Commission was given the task of approving applications for successor parish status. However, difficulties arose because the Government laid down restrictive guidelines to the effect that such an authority should not have more than 20,000 population or alternatively not more than one-fifth of the population of its parent district council. The intention was to forestall the creation of third-tier units sufficiently large and powerful to constitute a possible challenge to a district. As a result 133 applications were rejected while 269 were granted. This led to some parliamentary protest and an indication from the Government that some cases might be reconsidered.[8] A further review by the Boundary Commission based on a more flexible use of the guidelines produced a further twenty-seven successor councils. At the last moment another four applications were accepted. It can be argued not only that the guidelines were too restrictive but also that the Act should have permitted the establishment of third-tier parish-style councils with largely advisory powers in the wards of even the largest cities.

Where a former borough was not permitted to keep its separate third-tier council, the method of preserving its dignities depended on whether the second-tier authority for the area became a borough. If it did, the old charter rights and privileges transferred to the new and larger borough. Where the district is not a borough, district councillors representing the former borough become charter trustees entitled to hold land and to appoint one of their own number to be a town mayor. There are fifty bodies of charter trustees.

Other traditional civic dignities were retained. Mayors of the sixteen largest and most prestigious boroughs are entitled to the style 'Lord Mayor'. The Mayor of York has the special privilege of being 'the Right Honourable the Lord Mayor'. Forty-one English boroughs and the former Ely urban district were granted the designation City; this honour was often associated with the site of a cathedral. Windsor has the style of Royal Borough and Berkshire is a royal county. All the new authorities wished to retain the dignities which were traditional to their locality. All their applications to keep them were granted. Five cities, Chichester, Ely, Ripon, Truro and Wells, have become third-tier town authorities and here the status of city relates to the town and not the district. Salisbury and Lichfield have no separate third-tier authority so the title of City has been preserved through the use of charter trustees. At Rochester there are not even charter trustees as the former authority has been absorbed in a new borough with another name: tradition has been preserved by the issue of Letters Patent conferring the dignity on the area of the former city council.

These prerogatives affect the ceremonial rather than the practical aspects of local government. Nevertheless they arouse interest among councillors. Perhaps the rather exaggerated concern devoted to these niceties did something to mollify wounded susceptibilities in towns which lost status during the reorganisation. Certainly, the sponsors of the 1972 Act accepted that the promotion of good human relationships would play an important part in determining the success of the legislation. Newly elected councillors in the counties and districts were sent a free copy of the Bains Report[9] at government expense. A report on local administration in Sunderland[10] based on a study initiated by the DOE was a further attempt at ministerial education of local authorities which tried to persuade them to be more responsive and accessible to the public. Section 100 of the 1972 Act gave a general right to press and public to attend meetings of local authorities and their committees. Machinery for consultation with local authority staff in the period of reorganisation is discussed in Chapter 6. And the need for constant liaison between county and district authorities was stressed in the Bains Report.[11] Accordingly some new authorities have established permanent joint committees on which both county and districts are represented; these bodies cover either a whole county or an individual district. They review matters of common interest, particularly services that one authority provides for another, development plans and capital expenditure in the non-key sector. They facilitate meetings between officials and councillors from different authorities. And they can be valuable in fostering mutual co-operation and understanding. The importance of such harmony cannot be overstressed because of the close inter-relationship between the tasks which counties and districts have to perform.

Functions

Many major problems of reorganisation arose from the distribution of functions between the two main tiers. Some functions, notably planning and highways, are shared between them. Others with related problems, e.g. social services and housing, are divided between the tiers in the shire counties. Such a pattern must provide opportunities for mutual jealousy, conflict, buck-passing and frustration. Much of this would have been averted had the Royal Commission proposal for unitary authorities been adopted.

The case against unitary authorities was the manifest impossibility of delimiting areas suitable for all local authority services. To a degree, the matter is political although not necessarily in a party sense. The size of authority required for some services is so large that to build the whole of local administration upon such a base would produce a very strong feeling that local government had ceased to be local and that democratic values were being crushed by a new bureaucratic monolith. So the system of tiers, traditional in rural areas, still remains. The more expensive services tend to be allocated to the authorities with greater financial resources. Specialised services required by few people, or which demand the use of highly skilled staff in short supply, go to authorities with a substantial population. The top tier also has responsibility for services which are felt to require greatest uniformity or perhaps greatest supervision by the central government: the police are an obvious example. Second-tier authorities are given functions where local knowledge and responsiveness to local needs are felt to be important. Which of these criteria apply most forcibly to any particular service must be a matter of opinion. Spokesmen for counties and districts argued these matters at length before 1972 during the prolonged discussions on local government reform.

The following paragraphs describe the distribution of functions made by the Local Government Act 1972. The immediate purpose is to provide an outline of these arrangements. Detailed consideration of the major problems that arise from this allocation will be found in Chapters 4 and 5.

As noted above, the main difference between the metropolitan and the shire counties is that the latter are responsible for education, libraries and the social services while the former are not. It follows that the second-tier authorities are significantly more important in the metropolitan areas. Another distinction is that metropolitan counties are passenger transport authorities; in non-metropolitan areas this function is usually not a local government service but where it is the districts are responsible. However, all counties have the duty of promoting public transport policy in co-operation with bus operators and British Rail.

All counties are police and fire brigade authorities except that some counties are combined for police purposes. Consumer protection, including the inspection of weights and measures, food and drugs is another general field of county activity. Minor county duties are road safety and the provision of smallholdings. Some counties have special duties in connection with National Parks.

Other functions are shared between counties and districts, notably highways and planning. Counties are the highway authorities. However, districts can claim to maintain unclassified roads in urban areas, i.e. the areas of the former borough and urban district councils, subject to county financial control. So the actual distribution of work depends on local agreements. Counties are responsible for local traffic orders and control of parking, but districts have concurrent powers, with county consent, to provide off-street car parks. Town and country planning responsibilities are divided with counties preparing structure plans while districts draw up local plans which are to set out the detailed implications of county policy. Districts also decide whether to grant development permission, save where an application is of sufficient importance to raise issues which affect county policy, in which case the matter is remitted for decision by the county planning authority. Districts issue enforcement orders and revocations of planning permission. Both counties and districts have powers in relation to town development. Another example of shared responsibility relates to abandoned motor vehicles: districts remove them but counties destroy them. This is a particular application of the general principle that districts collect refuse and counties dispose of it. Other concurrent powers relate to recreation and leisure facilities, swimming baths, open spaces and entertainments, aerodromes and action in natural emergencies.

Districts have sole responsibility for environmental and public health services including building regulations, clean air, drainage and the inspection of offices, shops and factories. Housing is perhaps their most important duty. They collect the rates from the public and pay the precepts of the counties and parishes. Districts may operate buses where local powers existed before 1972; in addition they can subsidise services and finance travel concessions. They can provide allotments, markets and civic restaurants and are responsible for coast protection. In addition they are licensing authorities for theatres, cinemas, night refreshment houses and many other purposes.

Individual local authorities may obtain additional powers through Private Bill legislation. Otherwise local government is bound by a firm *ultra vires* rule which forbids the spending of public money other than in ways authorised by statute. Even so there is some flexibility in that a county, a district or a parish can spend up to the proceeds of a rate of 2p on any purpose which is in the interests of its area. Expenditure under this heading may include contributions to charity.

The allocation of functions in the 1972 Act involved some transfers between the two tiers. Registration of electors, local land charges and various licensing duties which were previously county responsibilities now adhere to the districts. Conversely, refuse disposal, traditionally a district task, was handed over to the counties. In other cases—and this applies to the major services—the extent of a particular authority's duties were often substantially changed. It was inevitable that this upheaval would create transitional problems. The Local Government Act 1972 attempted to ease this situation. Section 113 allowed the staff of one local authority to be placed at the disposal of another. Section 101 allowed one authority, subject to some exceptions, to request another authority to act on its behalf—to be its agent. The concept of agency is of considerable importance for it confers on the agent some measure of power to take decisions on how a service is to be managed. It was not intended solely as a means of easing problems of transition but was viewed as a method of fostering long-term co-operation between councils and of introducing some flexibility into the way in which their business was conducted. Equally, it is arguable that the idea of agency provides a fresh opportunity for conflict between counties and districts, for which the earlier experience of delegation arrangements provides an unhappy precedent.[12]

NOTES

1. There are also fourteen ex-urban areas that have parish councils.
2. Official documents use the terminology non-metropolitan counties and non-metropolitan districts.
3. In addition, aldermen disappeared. Before 1974 one-quarter of county and borough councils were aldermen elected for a six-year term of office by the councillors.
4. An exception to this rule is Christchurch in Dorset which is not a sparsely populated area. Here the intention was that Christchurch should be combined with Lymington to form a district of average size. But at a late stage of the Bill the House of Lords insisted that Lymington remain in Hampshire. So Christchurch was left to form a district on its own with a population of only 33,000.
5. In the Crawley/Horley area, pressure to alter the West Sussex/Surrey boundary continued after the 1972 Act had been passed. The Horley and Charlwood Act 1974 subsequently reduced the area transferred to West Sussex.
6. DOE Circular 51/73 gave advice to local authorities on the making of these applications.
7. See p. 18 *infra* for an explanation of charter trustees. Crosby and Sefton were too large to be third-tier authorities.
8. HL Deb., Vol. 345, cols 263–80.
9. The nature and significance of the Bains Report is discussed below, pp. 28–46.
10. The study was undertaken by McKinsey and Co. Inc. in collaboration with the Sunderland County Borough Council and published in two volumes, *A Basic Handbook* and *A Working Guide* (HMSO, 1973).
11. See pp. 93–4.
12. Peter G. Richards, *Delegation in Local Government* (Allen & Unwin, 1956). For further discussion of agency see Ch. 4 *infra*.

Chapter 2

PREPARATORY WORK BY
FORMER AUTHORITIES

The Joint Committees

There were two major stages in the transition from the old local authorities to the new. First, the existing councils within a new authority's area were brought together by the establishment of a joint committee under the terms of Section 264 of the 1972 Local Government Act. Second, the members of the new authorities were elected well in advance of the actual handover date. County elections were held on 15 March 1973; metropolitan district elections were held on 12 April 1973; other district councils were elected on 7 June 1973.[1] So in the counties the old and new councils existed side by side for over a year before the start of the new system. Even in the non-metropolitan districts the new councillors had over nine months to get ready.

The whole framework of preparation, in fact, evolved over a much longer period. Councillors elected to the new authorities found that much detailed spadework had already been done by their predecessors through the medium of the joint committees authorised by the 1972 Act. It is arguable that too much work had been done, that new councils were rushed or conditioned into ratifying decisions framed by people whose democratic mandate had virtually expired. The purpose of this chapter is to examine the work of these preliminary joint committees and to consider their influence over the new authorities.

Section 264 of the 1972 Act laid down the duties of the joint committees and authorised the Secretary of State to adjudicate in any local disputes about the balance of representation on these bodies as between existing councils. There were few such disputes. Indeed, the general pattern was for committees covering the proposed new counties and metropolitan districts to have been at work on a voluntary basis for several months before the 1972 Bill reached the Statute Book. Then when the Bill became an Act the voluntary bodies acquired statutory status. In some areas a very early start had been made. Bradford County Borough called a meeting of authorities to be included in the new Bradford Metropolitan District in September 1971 based on the proposals in Circular 8/71 and before the text of the actual Bill had been published. However, most of the other authorities concerned felt that any action would be premature and no progress was made for three months.

These early meetings in the shires were often between county and county borough representatives, with county districts joining in later. Such anticipation was not always possible in the case of non-metropolitan districts for here some boundaries were uncertain until after the Bill became law. Where boundaries were virtually unchanged there was little for the joint committee to do. For the Manchester Metropolitan District, enlarged by the addition of one parish, only a single meeting of the joint committee was needed. Coventry, which absorbed two parishes, found no need at all for a committee. At the other extreme, the former West Riding of Yorkshire was involved in committees for two metropolitan counties, five shire counties and nine metropolitan districts. The few counties which suffered no geographical change did appoint joint committees to consider relationships with the reorganised districts.

This chapter is based on a study of the reports of joint committees for the new county and metropolitan district councils.[2] It is not a statistical survey because a few authorities, mainly districts, failed to respond to requests for information; because the reports themselves are uneven in character with some containing more detail than others; because a numerical analysis could be misleading since proposals different in form can be similar in intention and vice versa. Thus the survey is somewhat impressionistic and the examples quoted tend to illustrate exceptions rather than a general trend.

The basic tasks of the joint committees were to arrange for the election of the new councils and to facilitate transition from the old to the new. This involved research, co-ordination and an element of education of the incoming councillors. Thus the joint committees made recommendations about future committee and departmental structures; they also brought together officials in order to collate information which would assist the harmonisation of policies, systems and procedures. In addition, they considered proposals by existing authorities which might be contrary to the interests of the new council, e.g. in regard to the appointment or grading of staff. Expenses of these committees were to be shared between the constituent authorities on whatever basis was agreed between them or, failing such agreement, cost allocation was to be determined by the Secretary of State.

The general willingness to proceed with the preparatory work is indicative of a general acceptance of the reform. However, the picture is not wholly one of smooth co-operation. In order to buttress their claim to remain separate and independent, the Isle of Wight County Council did not join in the work of the new Hampshire Joint Committee although there was some liaison at officer level. Initially the former East Riding County Council failed to join the Joint Committee for the new North Yorkshire. And the disputes surrounding the establishment of Avon caused the preliminary work there to be interrupted.

It is important to stress that senior officials played a large part in the work of the joint committees. Normally they accompanied elected representatives to the meetings and attended as their advisers. Detailed consideration of the problems of transition was remitted to working groups which commonly comprised the chief officers of the constituent authorities who had responsibility for a particular function. Where these working groups produced agreement, the parent joint committee could be expected to ratify the conclusions reached. The role of the elected representatives became critical where working parties failed to reach agreement, perhaps through institutional or even personal rivalry. There is no doubt that this preparatory work proved more difficult in areas in which there was no dominant geographical centre and, therefore, there was room for dispute over where the joint committee should meet, for such a decision could have an influence on where the new authority should meet and where new administrative headquarters should be sited. So counties like Leicester and Nottingham which have an unchallenged centre were spared a source of tension which affected counties where the location of new administrative headquarters aroused competing claims and loyalties, as in Cambridgeshire and Hereford and Worcester.

As the joint committees' task was, in essence, preparatory, their main function was to explore problem areas and suggest solutions rather than make firm decisions. There were, however, some matters that did require a decision for the new authorities to start their formal existence. An official had to be nominated to summon the first meeting of a new council: usually the person chosen was the Clerk of the former council or, in the case of an amalgamation, the Clerk of the largest of the authorities being merged. Persons had to be nominated to undertake the tasks of Chairman and Vice-Chairman of the new authority until the newly elected councillors could choose their chairman, i.e. it was necessary to arrange for someone to preside at the initial election of chairman of the new bodies. Decisions had to be made as to where and when the new council should meet and an agenda for its first meeting had to be formulated.[3] Also the joint committees decreed a set of standing orders to be followed at the first meeting of the fledgeling councils; usually these were the standing orders of the local authority whose Clerk had been chosen to give initial service to the new authority. Transitional arrangements were also made to provide legal, financial and secretarial support for the new authorities until such time as they appointed their own staff.

With these trivial exceptions, the role of the joint committee was to prepare and advise. They were consulted by the Home Office on the warding arrangements for the first elections of the new councils. They were consulted by the DOE on names for the new authorities. Their views were invited on whether successor parish councils should be established for places that were to lose their separate urban status. The Staff Commission invited their opinions on the procedure that should govern the appointment of staff. Above all, the joint committees provided advice for the new authorities. DOE Circular 68/72 was careful to point out the limitations that the joint committees must observe. 'Being essentially advisory bodies, however, they will wish to distinguish between the interim and preparatory work which properly falls to the joint committees and the policy decisions which must of necessity await settlement by the new councils after they have been elected.'[4] The Circular went on to stress that the new councils must take the crucial decisions about management structure; equally, the joint committees should consider the Bains Report and make suggestions as to how its ideas might be applied locally. Further, the joint committees should study the accommodation position, prepare information about existing staff establishments, review the extent to which common services might be shared after 1 April 1974, list contracts of the existing councils due to run beyond 1 April 1974 and collate details of the appointments made by existing councils to outside bodies. In addition the Circular suggested that the joint committees should be used by existing authorities as a means to harmonise policies in relation to capital investment, capital commitments, proposals to sell or purchase land, staff regrading and the standardisation of work procedures. Clearly, early co-operation on these matters would smooth the path of the changeover.

The detail covered in the formal reports of the joint committees varied greatly. The Durham Joint Committee produced a modest cyclostyled document of thirty-eight quarto pages. Neighbouring Cumbria published a massive tome of 908 foolscap-size printed pages. These reports reflect the contrast between the two areas. Although Durham was absorbing the county borough of Darlington and a rural district formerly in the North Riding, the character of the county remained unchanged. For many years it had been a Labour stronghold: it was certain that the political control would be unchanged. So the outgoing authorities knew they would be handing over in name only. Policies, and many councillors, would be the same. Cumbria provides a total contrast. It is composed of two former counties, two former county boroughs and small parts of two other counties. There could be no sense of continuity as in Durham. There was also also no dominant political group and no certainty that one would arise. In both practical and psychological terms, the task of paving the way for a new administration was much greater. The response in Cumbria was a report from the Joint Committee which proposed in much detail how the new county should set about its work.

A few joint committees were somewhat uncertain and tentative in their recommendations. At one extreme some reports made proposals that were not necessary or perhaps appropriate. The Tameside document, although very clearly presented, belonged to the hesitant category. 'So far as departmental structure is concerned, the Joint Committee conclude that it was not expedient to make recommendations upon the matters to be determined ... It is their view that the Council will require time to consider what its final committee structure shall be and will want to have the advice of its Chief Executive Officer.' The Bedfordshire Joint Committee presented the new authority with alternative proposals for a management structure prepared by chief officials from the existing county and the Luton County Borough. At the other extreme the Stockport Joint Committee advised the new council to start its meetings with prayers and to apply for borough status. One might think that such questions could be decided by the new councillors without parental guidance.

Management Structures—the Bains Report
The task of the joint committees—and the range of their probable influence—was substantially widened by the publication of the Bains Report. This document was the result of a joint venture by the DOE and the four main local authority associations, and was designed to offer advice to the new councils on their management and organisation. A steering committee was formed under the

chairmanship of Sir Frank Marshall, then chairman of the Association of Municipal Corporations, and consisted largely of representatives from the local authority associations: the detailed recommendations were produced by a working group headed by Mr Bains, then Clerk of the Kent County Council. The injection of the Report into the other preparations for reorganisation virtually required the joint committees to make wider recommendations about future management and organisation than they might otherwise have thought necessary.

The Bains Report developed a managerial philosophy of the kind which had become increasingly acceptable to elected representatives, at least in the larger authorities. This recognised that the scale of local government activity was so wide that councillors could not hope to control detail. Instead, they must perforce limit themselves to making major decisions on policy and avoid dealing with individual policies and grievances. The Bains Report argued that the functions of councillors and officials were not separated into watertight compartments. So officials had to concern themselves with policy while councillors might sometimes intervene in administration. The Report noted that the nature of a councillor's interest in local government varied between individuals. Some were mainly attracted to welfare work; others to restricting expenditure; others to management, often on commercial lines; others to general service to the community. The Report added: 'Other categories can no doubt be identified', but was too tactful to proceed further.

Such an analysis of councillor motivation fitted neatly the proposal that a local authority should have a senior or central committee to formulate main objectives and priorities and oversee all the authority's activities. However, this central committee was not to have a monopoly of policy-making because some decisions would be left to functional committees that have general supervision over their own programme areas. The central committee, the Policy and Resources Committee, should be advised by a Chief Executive, the top official of the local authority. This officer should not be required to have any specific professional qualification, so leaving the field for recruitment wide open. To keep his mind and his desk free to deal with major issues he should not, the Bains Report argued, have departmental responsibilities. Nor should he have a deputy. Instead, he should be assisted by a management team, a kind of Cabinet formed from the more important officers. The existence of the management team, Bains proposed, should be formally recognised by the local authority. Inter-disciplinary teams of officials should also be formed to advise the various committees. This suggestion, and the parallel recommendation that committee responsibilities should not be allocated on a simple functional basis, were both designed to check the development of separate departmental empires and loyalties based on the provision of particular services. Thus there should be a corporate approach to management rather than a departmental approach.

Circular 68/72 from the DOE had urged the local joint committees to consider the Bains Report while stressing that final decisions on management structures could be made only by the new councils. Nevertheless, it was clear that if detailed suggestions were presented to the new authorities they were likely to have a strong influence on the final outcome. The elected representatives on the joint committees looked to their staff for advice and duly received comments on Bains from working groups of their chief officers. In some places, notably Essex, the chief officers anticipated Bains by working out their own ideas in advance of the publication of the Bains Report. In general, both officers and elected representatives gave Bains a favourable reception. The theory of corporate management became an accepted orthodoxy. Perhaps the doctrine was accepted too uncritically. The emphasis in the thinking of the joint committees tended to be in terms of the need to ensure co-operation between the various parts of a local authority's organisation, to avoid separatism and the evils of departmentalism. Some attention was also given to the question of which chief officers should be regular members of the management team. Little thought seemed to be given to the practical effects of corporate management in terms of the influence of officials or on future relationships between members and officials. What happens if the management team fails to agree? Do councillors get conflicting advice? The Bains view of this problem was: 'Generally speaking we would expect such reports to be unanimous, but provision should be made for a strongly held minority view to be presented.' This is a neat formula for flexibility but it still does not explain how the unanimous view is to emerge. Will the management team achieve unity like a British Cabinet, or like the Cabinet of the United States where the President must prevail? Is the Chief Executive Prime Minister or President? There has been a general disposition to tactfully ignore these issues. Exceptionally, Rotherham Joint Committee solved the problem by refusing to agree to the concept of a permanent management team.

In spite of the substantial and undoubted influence of the Bains Report, the ideas on future management that emerged from the joint committees were by no means uniform. Only one shire county, Hertfordshire, failed to accept the concept of a single, central policy

committee. The Hertfordshire plan was for two central committees, a Finance and Resources Committee and a Co-ordinating
Committee 'concerned with the formulation of Council policy on
issues, other than the allocation of resources, affecting the Council
as a whole or calling for effective co-ordination of the Council's services'. In Essex a Co-ordinating and Finance Committee was
proposed which was to deal with resource allocation and areas of
policy that concern more than one committee: this is a weaker role
for the central committee than that envisaged by Bains.

For the service committees there was a general stress on their
importance in policy formation; no doubt this was due to a desire to
avoid any feeling that councillors serving on these committees were
second-class in relation to councillors on the central policy committee. The more cautious approach to a Policy and Resources
Committee was well expressed by the South Tyneside Joint Committee:

'The relationship of such a Committee with the other Committees of
the Council and with the Council itself is a matter of some delicacy.
It is of importance that the Council meeting should be, and should
be seen to be, the place where the final decision on major matters is
taken. At the same time the functional Committees should not be
made to feel that decisions concerning their business is (sic) being
usurped by another Committee. The over-riding function of the
Policy and Resources Committee is to co-ordinate and experience
has shown that this function can best be fulfilled by their views
being expressed to the Council in the form of recommendations and
advice rather than decisions. The Council is then free to consider
the resolutions of the functional committees simultaneously with the
advice of the Policy and Resources Committee and take a final
decision.'[5]

This statement expresses orthodox democratic theory. However,
where a council is under firm party control, one assumes that any
conflict between committees would be settled in advance and in
private within the caucus of the majority party.

There was a general acceptance of the idea that minority parties
should be represented on the central policy committee. On this issue
the Labour Party softened its attitude. The Party had opposed the
view of the Maud Committee that political minorities should be
included in the membership of the Management Boards on the
grounds that officers were likely to be inhibited in giving advice to a
politically divided committee and that councillors from the majority

group might avoid presenting conflicting views in the presence of their opponents. If a group met separately and informally before the official committee meetings they might come to decisions without the benefit of advice from officials. So the Labour view was that where a local authority worked on political lines, the key policy committee, like the Cabinet, must be a one-party body. However, the Bains Report recommended that 'the advice of officers must be available wherever effective decisions are taken by members', and this formula opened the possibility that officials might attend party groups of councillors. This weakened the Labour objection to a multi-party policy committee. The Leeds Joint Committee reflected the changed Labour attitude by proposing that the advice of chief officers be available to each party group of councillors and that, subject to this condition, the Policy and Resources Committee should be multi-party. But not all Labour controlled authorities followed this line: Gateshead, with an overwhelming Labour majority, was one exception.

The Bains Report produced a model committee structure consisting of a central Policy Resources Committee with four sub-committees together with a limited number of committees concerned with a particular service or programme area. The number of the latter would depend upon the powers of an authority but should not exceed six. Here the joint committees often departed from Bains by suggesting more service committees. It was felt either that a particular activity was so important as to require a separate committee or, alternatively, there was a general view that each councillor should be entitled to serve on at least two committees and that it was better to achieve this through more committees rather than having over-large committees. The view in Manchester, dominated by the Labour Party, was clearly conservative:

'We consider that ... members of a committee and their chairmen in particular tend to become expert in the work of their committee; we also consider that providing this specialisation does not narrow the field within which the members tend to concern themselves and thereby prevent them from acquiring a corporate view of the objectives of the Corporation as a whole, this specialisation can and does lead to the efficient operation of the Corporation. We do not see any virtue in limiting for limitations sake the number of committees nor are we averse to having a committee dealing with the work of a particular department.[6]

The new Manchester authority proceeded to establish fifteen main committees, and in at least six counties or metropolitan districts at least ten main committees were nominated. The Bains plan for four sub-committees of the Policy and Resources Committee was accepted only by a minority. The four proposed were Finance, Personnel, Land and Performance Review. The Performance Review Sub-committee, according to the Bains Report, should monitor the performance of a local authority by comparing its achievements with its objectives. To use a parliamentary analogy, a local authority should have its own Public Accounts Committee. This idea proved to be either too sophisticated or too embarrassing for many of the local joint committees and they generally contented themselves with three sub-committees of the central policy committee.[7]

More acceptable was the concept of a Chief Executive Officer and all counties and metropolitan districts subsequently made such an appointment. However, there was some hesitation about the name and feeling of nostalgia for the traditional name, Clerk. In this case the formality of a title does have practical implications. The Bains view was that the Chief Executive should not be responsible for the legal and secretarial servicing of committees. In Essex, where the style of Chief Executive and Clerk was adopted, this official is designated as Clerk to the Committees of the Council. The central issue here is whether the Chief Executive should have a department of a traditional type or whether a separate chief officer, a Secretary to the council, should perform duties associated in the past with the office of Clerk. The Bains view, fashionable among management theorists for some time, was that the Chief Executive should be saved from the cares of running a large department, otherwise he has no time and energy to 'think big' about the problems of his authority. The alternative argument is that without a department the Chief Executive could easily become isolated, starved of information and generally out-of-touch with immediate problems. The burden of responsibility associated with a traditional Clerk's department can be minimised by substantial delegation of authority. A department, if properly organised, should be a source of support for a Chief Executive, not a drag upon him. Most joint committees followed the Bains approach rather than the Essex pattern. Others, like Cheshire, left the issue open to be settled by the new council in conjunction with the advice of the Chief Executive. Where a County Clerk or Town Clerk was expected to become the Chief Executive of the new authority one assumes that his influence on this particular matter was substantial, for individuals have strong and quite different preferences about work-styles. The Cheshire report, although stating fairly the conflicting positions, was somewhat tilted against Bains. It is not surprising that the Chief Executive in Cheshire, in effect, leads a traditional department.

When a Chief Executive has no department the status of the Secretary to the local authority is greatly enhanced. He will be a leading member of the management team responsible for the smooth operation of routine administration. Where the Chief Executive has a department the Secretary becomes a member of it. He may or may not be a member of the management team, and his role may depend more on reputation and personal relationships than formal job specifications.

The relationship between the Chief Executive and other chief officials was a sensitive matter. The Bains Report included a job specification for a Chief Executive which gave him 'authority over all other officers as far as this is necessary for the efficient management and execution of the council's functions'.[8] This formulation raises the question whether a Chief Executive could over-rule a chief officer on a matter which lay clearly within the latter's professional expertise. And who is to decide if there is dispute about what is necessary for efficient management? Is the Chief Executive to be judge in his own cause? Some joint committees accepted the Bains job specification in toto: others chose to ignore the issue.

A closely related matter was the control of staffing. The Bains Report stressed the importance of personnel work and manpower planning. It advocated that the Personnel Officer be responsible directly to the Chief Executive and not be subordinated to any other chief officer. Probably this weakens the position of a chief officer in relation to the staffing establishment of his own department: nevertheless a high degree of independence for the Personnel Officer is a necessary consequence of corporate management. Most joint committees followed the Bains proposal but a few placed the Personnel Officer under the Director of Administration or Secretary, presumably to keep the desk of the Chief Executive as clear as possible. There was also discussion, not reflected in the joint committee reports, as to whether enough personnel officers of adequate calibre were available to fill the role assigned to them.

Bains's advice that deputy chief officers were often unnecessary was ignored almost everywhere. There was a universal feeling that someone must be recognised as in charge whenever a chief officer was away. The involvement of chief officers in the management team also strengthened the case for a second-in-command. Naturally, senior staff opposed the elimination of deputies as this would have had a serious effect on career prospects. So the tradition of deputies

was retained. However, where it was proposed that a Chief Executive should be free of departmental cares, no deputy Chief Executive was envisaged, but the joint committees made various suggestions as to who should take his place in his absence.

Formal recognition of a management team of selected chief
officers was generally acceptable to joint committees although
Rotherham resisted the idea that such a body would meet regularly.
The delicate question was which of the chief officers should be
regular members of the management team. In the shire counties the
usual composition was Chief Executive, Treasurer, Director of
Education, Engineer, Director of Social Services and the Planning
Officer with possible additions of the Architect, Solicitor or Secretary and Estates Officer. (The titles vary from one authority to
another.) The metropolitan counties typically have a smaller team
with the Chief Executive, Treasurer, Solicitor or Secretary,
Engineer, Planner and Director of Passenger Transport. In metropolitan districts the composition is more diverse because of varying
patterns of appointment of chief officers in the field of planners /
architects / engineers and surveyors. But in addition to the chief
officer from this general area the management team was recommended to include the Chief Executive (of course), Treasurer,
Director of Education, Director of Social Services and possibly the
Solicitor or Secretary, Director of Housing and Director of
Recreation or Leisure. It is notable that the Chief Constable was
not thought of as a member of the management team.

For departmental structures, the Bains Report presented alternatives. One was the continuation of the traditional arrangement in
which each main sector of a local authority's work has a separate
department headed by a chief officer. The alternative was to group
allied activities under the supervision of a Director: thus in a shire
the Director of Technical Services might have overall responsibility
for planning, engineering, transportation, architecture, valuation
and estate management. No doubt all these matters are inter-
dependent but the concept of multi-faced departments did not win
acceptance. Perhaps the various professions within local government were even keener to retain separate departments than councillors were desirous of keeping separate committees. Nevertheless, the
outcome was not uniform and in many places the number of departments was reduced. In particular, there was great variation in the
treatment of the library service. Sometimes it becomes a sub-section
of education; sometimes it is grouped under recreation and leisure
services including parks; sometimes the library, together with
museums and art galleries, forms a separate department. The major

innovation is that of the department of the Secretary, Solicitor or Director of Administration which embraces legal and secretarial services; this is a consequence of deciding that a Chief Executive should be free from departmental responsibilities.

The Bains Report also made reference to the need in some areas to arrange for an element of decentralisation to bring services to the place of need, to provide a convenient point of public access to local authority organisation and to allow for optimum deployment of resources. The need for area offices is greater in the larger local authorities—larger either in terms of population or size. In Cumbria the Joint Committee paid particular attention to this problem, no doubt because the population of this county tends to be dispersed round its edges. Its Report suggested criteria which should determine the pattern of area organisation; they covered service to the public, the need to co-operate with district councils, the operational requirements of each county service and the need for liaison between county services. These criteria led to conflicting solutions. The need to work together with districts suggested that county area organisation should coincide with district boundaries, with perhaps a county area unit embracing the whole of more than one district. Functional requirements might be best served by ignoring district boundaries. After considerable discussion and some disagreement it was proposed that education, social services, libraries and consumer protection be decentralised on the basis of four areas that followed district council boundaries, but that highways, transportation and the fire service also be decentralised but on a different pattern. Thus in the latter group the technical requirements of the service were given greater weight in deciding the pattern of organisation.

Recognition of the need for area organisation was not, however, restricted to the more sparsely populated areas. At Leeds the Joint Committee proposed the establishment of principal offices throughout the metropolitan district together with sub-offices for some purposes, e.g. the social services. There is no doubt that such decentralisation is convenient for the public as it provides easier access for those with problems or complaints, particularly in the case of the county services which were excluded from the possibility of agency arrangements under the 1972 Act, i.e. education and the social services. In the latter case, the development of local offices and of teams of social workers covering a limited geographical area is a well established practice. Councillors are naturally interested in issues of decentralisation in relation to cost and the convenience and quality of service offered to the public. Nevertheless, there is no element here of conflict between authorities—as with agency—and the number of area offices and the nature of their relationship to their own headquarters are less likely to excite widespread public debate.

However, local government seems to be able to provide an exception to almost every general rule. In Hampshire the main dispute facing the Joint Committee was not over agency or over how the county boroughs of Portsmouth and Southampton could preserve their identity. Instead, it was the question of whether the county education service should be based on four or eight areas. The eight unit plan allowed Portsmouth and Southampton to keep their own separate identities as areas: under the four unit scheme they were to be combined with surrounding areas. The usual expectation would be that such towns would wish to retain their exclusiveness as far as possible and that in such circumstances they would favour the eight area scheme. But this was not so, particularly in Southampton. The argument was that with four areas, each area could have its own team of educational advisers, whereas with eight areas the advisers would have to be unified under the control of county headquarters. Thus the issue was not simply one about the number of area offices but about the extent of their functions and, therefore, of their staff. An administrative officer controlling a team of specialist advisers would clearly command a higher status and salary than one who did not. Detailed arguments were submitted to the Hampshire Joint Committee for and against the four and eight unit schemes. Proposed arrangements in other counties were collected and introduced into the argument. Inevitably the Committee failed to make any recommendation and, very properly, the matter was left for the new county authority to decide. In the meantime opinions were canvassed from local authorities, teachers' organisations and the staff and governors or managers of individual schools. This incident illustrates that where professional officers fail to agree, the questions are resolved in a wider forum. The elected representative faced with conflicting advice has to adjudicate. Where the advice placed before him is consensual, it is easy, perhaps too easy, to accept it.

Agency arrangements were an inevitable source of conflict. Here were strong pressures working against agreement in the working parties of chief officials. Upon these decisions depended the future status and importance of chief officials of the new district councils. Indeed, the issue often became whether certain sections of departments were to be transferred from a district to the county with implications for the provision of office accommodation, increase in travelling time and disturbance to the domestic life of local government staff. So it is not surprising that the working parties sometimes failed to agree on agency—either on its extent or conditions or on whether it should exist at all. These disagreements were then reported to the joint committees. If no solution was found at this level, the matter was then passed on to the new authorities. The various stages of discussion each helped to moderate views and many local issues were ironed out at officer level at a fairly early stage. The total situation was infinitely complex and patchy. In some areas basic agreements were reached perhaps between officers or between elected representatives sometimes working in a party context. Alternatively, the conflict could be wide-ranging or be restricted to a particular service or particular locality. A full discussion of agency will be found in Chapter 4.

Concurrent powers pose a similar problem to agency in that they invite a head-on clash between county and district over the distribution of functions. The list of concurrent powers in the 1972 Act is surprisingly long: it includes museums and art galleries, the acquisition of land for planning purposes, clearance of derelict land, aerodromes, provision of caravan sites, health education, provision for recreation and tourism including country parks, swimming baths and entertainments, and powers to deal with natural emergencies. Some joint committees made recommendations as to how these responsibilities should be shared out.

There was considerable concern that the new authorities should work closely together. Councillors from the county boroughs, unused to the two-tier arrangement, were keen to insist that counties and districts must co-operate; in many areas the joint committees preparing the handover recommended that the new authorities should establish regular county-district liaison through joint committees. Kent, in particular, gave much thought to the creation of such bodies. One view was that county-district committees should be formed for each district area and perform an advisory function over the whole range of local government services. The authorities which had formerly exercised delegated education powers pressed for separate advisory committees for education. It was argued that the churches and teachers' representatives should join area education committees whereas they would be quite out of place on a body with a general advisory brief. Further, the volume of business concerned with education would be so great as to overburden all-purpose committees. On the other hand, it was claimed that separate functional committees should be avoided or otherwise the whole corporate approach to management might be undermined with each main sector of local government stressing its peculiar needs and identity.

Problems relating to a particular local authority function were examined by working parties of chief officers. Normally they reported to the parent joint committee through a steering committee of clerks or clerks and treasurers. The steering committees were sometimes needed to hold in check the specialised enthusiasm of a professional group. Thus at Kirklees the Clerk's Steering Committee was severely critical of the education working party because it felt that the latter was attempting to establish a semi-autonomous education department within the new authority. In general, the efforts of these working parties were scarcely reflected in many of the final joint committee reports to the new councils. Partly this was because much of the discussion was technical and detailed; partly it raised questions about the harmonisation of policy that could be properly decided only by the new elected councillors.

On financial matters the joint committees surveyed the questions which demanded early decision by the new authorities. The extent of positive recommendations varied. In some areas the joint committees made specific proposals about the appointment of bankers, insurers and how the choice should be made between district audit and professional audit. Joint committees considered major development schemes by their constituent authorities which had major implications for future programmes of capital expenditure. Computer facilities were reviewed and their adequacy for the new authority assessed: sometimes support was given to a scheme for a new installation by one of the present authorities. The working parties of treasurers undertook a considerable amount of preparation for the assimilation of sometimes diverse financial systems of councils due to amalgamate. Included here were such matters as the details of financial control, methods of banking cash, central purchasing, and whether loans for house purchase should be made under the Small Dwellings Acquisition Act 1899 or the Housing Act 1958.

Accommodation for the new authority was everywhere an important issue and sometimes the dominating issue. At one level the problem was to slot departments into existing offices in a way most convenient for the staff and the public. Where existing space was not sufficient enquiries were started into where extra space might be found. At a second and grander level, plans were put forward for new headquarters for the new authority, e.g. the Berkshire plan for new offices at Shinfield Park. At a third level there was major disagreement as to where the new headquarters should be sited as in Hereford and Worcester: in such circumstances the decision had to be remitted to the new council.

The joint committees also gave considerable attention to information services and publicity and were encouraged to do so by DOE Circular 50/73. Everywhere the joint committees were asked for an opinion on whether poll cards should be provided for the initial elections for the new councils. (For subsequent elections poll cards are a statutory requirement.) Some joint committees urged that poll cards be provided: elsewhere they accepted advice from officials that it would be difficult to provide this facility in the time available. There was a general desire to assist public understanding of local government activities and wide support for the Bains proposal that the new authorities should appoint information officers. At Gateshead the Joint Committee appointed a public relations firm to spread information about their activities. All over the country internal 'house' bulletins were issued to keep local government staff in touch with the planning of reorganisation. Many joint committees also supported the Bains recommendation that basic secretarial services be provided for councillors to assist them in the task of keeping in touch with their constituents.

Inevitably the reorganisation of structure had an unsettling effect on local government staffs, worried about job prospects or future location of employment. The joint committees attempted to provide some reassurance through local consultative machinery both for office workers and outdoor staff by disseminating information about the general preparatory work being undertaken. Through the working parties of chief officers some joint committees assembled estimates of their future staff requirements, partly in order to obtain a clearer view of the likely extent of staff accommodation problems. But such figures could be no more than estimates because the standards of service to be provided was a major policy question that could be decided only by the newly elected councils. In some departments the staffing establishment depended heavily on the existence or extent of agency arrangements which again could be finally determined only by the new councils.

However, the joint committees did take some positive steps in relation to staff appointments. They vetted proposals by constituent authorities to make senior appointments which would have implications for the new authority. Many vacancies were left unfilled especially where a position was due to disappear on reorganisation day. There were also discussions about the payment of additional remuneration to officials not eligible for overtime pay in compensation for additional work necessitated by the reorganisation. At Gateshead the Joint Committee discussed the difficulties created by the Ryton UDC when it refused to make additional payments.

Many joint committees were consulted by the Staff Commission on the area from which the staff of the new authority should be recruited.[9] They received from the Staff Commission the names and addresses of local government officers who wished to be considered for appointment as Chief Executive of the new authority. The joint committees then had a choice as to what to do with this list of applicants.[10] The simplest course was to pass the list on to the new council but an alternative was to send out detailed application forms together with particulars of the post making it clear that the particulars were subject to confirmation by the new council. The latter procedure had the advantage of potentially saving time and speeding up the process of selection of the Chief Executive; the disadvantage was that the joint committee became involved in framing a job specification for the top post of which the new council might disapprove. In fact, where joint committees did choose to press ahead there is little evidence that their initiative caused subsequent difficulties. They could also invite applications for other chief officer posts from within the restricted recruitment area fixed by the Staff Commission but such action was again subject to the difficulty that job descriptions had to be provisional. Exceptionally, agreement was obtained from the Staff Commission that a particular chief officer post might be advertised nationally owing to a probable shortage of suitable applicants within the standard catchment area.

It is not possible to describe the variety of local topics, including the effects of local legislation, that cropped up in reports of joint committees. There was great interest in civic dignities, notably the preparation of armorial bearings for the new authority, while in districts in urban areas the prospect of application for borough status was often mentioned. Attention was also paid to future relationships with other bodies including the associations of local authorities, health and water authorities and towns abroad which had 'twinning' relationships with existing local councils. And perhaps a major contribution of the joint committees came from the mere fact of their existence. Each constituted an embryo for a new authority which had to grow rapidly and sometimes painfully to achieve maturity by 1 April 1974 when perforce it accepted responsibility for the operation of local government services.

The Influence of Joint Committees
The most significant section of each joint committee report was that devoted to the management structure of the new authority. Without doubt the Bains Report had a substantial impact on these proposals

although in many areas preparatory thinking, often on similar lines, was under way before the Report was published. No other official report has had such a rapid country-wide impact on local decisions. Certainly the acceptance of Bains's ideas was less than universal, but a study of the creation of the new authorities must enquire why this Report gained such prestige.

The Bains Report reflected a tide of opinion about local government which had been flowing steadily for some years. Its precursor, the Maud Committee Report of 1967, had prepared the way by stimulating local authorities to look afresh at their organisation, although the central concept of this Committee, that of a Management Board composed of councillors, failed to find any local support. Nevertheless Maud did succeed in making many local councils accept the need for more delegation to committees and to officers, combined with a check on departmentalism. There was a fair willingness to agree with the Maud diagnosis of the ills of local management methods even if the remedy offered was too unpalatable to be swallowed. Bains profited from Maud not merely in that the latter had performed a valuable educational function amongst local councillors, but also, by their experience of local reaction to Maud, the Bains group knew that no proposals were likely to become effective unless they provided what seemed to be a worthwhile field of activity for all elected representatives. So Bains allowed the functional or programme committees a share in policy and decision-making whereas Maud had sought to relegate them to an advisory role.

The outstanding feature of the support for Bains was its heterogeneous nature. The Department of the Environment, the associations of local authorities, the major political parties, and many leading elected representatives and local officials were in sympathy. There was a remarkable consensus that in broad outline Bains had shown what needed to be done to make the new authorities work with tolerable efficiency. This atmosphere was intensified by a fairly substantial campaign to sell the Bains package. Members of the Bains Committee addressed meetings throughout the country. A senior official from the Conservative Central Office addressed private party meetings of prominent Conservatives to support Bains. The Transport House discussion paper *Party, Councillors and Management*, circulated for the Labour Party's Local Government Conference at Newcastle in February 1973, also gave backing to the central Bains theme of the need for corporate management. No doubt the major parties felt that it would be easier for a local majority caucus to exercise firm control over a large new local authority were a central policy committee to be established which could then supervise administration through a chief executive assisted by a management team co-ordinating departmental actions. The party writ could be made to run more easily through a centralised system. It is notable that while the Labour Party document was critical of various details of the Bains recommendations there was support for the crucial unifying concepts—a Policy and Resources Committee, a Chief Executive and the general philosophy of corporate management.

Enthusiasm for Bains from the DOE and the associations of local authorities may have had a conflicting rationale. Both sides saw the Report as a contribution to more efficient local administration. Whitehall also hoped it would assist economy in expenditure and that the restraint on the independence of local authority departments would facilitate negotiations between the civil service and local councils. The associations felt that more efficient and larger units of local government should be more self-reliant and better able to withstand pressures from Whitehall. It was also acknowledged that the procedures used in many of the smaller authorities in 1972 would be quite unsuitable for the new councils. Larger authorities had already taken action to streamline their methods of business after the publication of the Maud Report and were ready to move further along this road. Elected representatives, especially the younger ones, accepted the need to surrender control over detail to officials in order to reduce demands on their time to acceptable limits and to enable them to concentrate attention on the more important issues.

Senior staff of local authorities welcomed the Bains assertion that they should be given wider powers to make decisions within the ambit of policy agreed by a council or a committee. Such procedure would speed up administration by obviating the need for minor items to be submitted to councillors before action could be taken. More discretion for officials improves their status and enhances their self-esteem. Bains's insistence on the need for co-ordination had become orthodox management theory. It was fully familiar to higher ranking administrative staff, many of whom had attended courses organised by the Institute of Local Government at the University of Birmingham which had preached for years the gospel of the collective approach to management. The concept of a management team also permitted the more important chief officers to share in consideration of the overall policy of their authority, a perspective previously limited to Clerks and Treasurers. Admittedly, in return, there was some loss of departmental independence. Chief officers excluded from the management team (and their immediate subordinates) were the most likely amongst local government officers to resist the concept of collective management. The precise composition of the management team became a delicate question, aggravated further because it had implications for salary levels.[11] But this type of friction was little publicised.

Vocal objections to the new style of management did come from some elected representatives, particularly the more elderly who perhaps suffered less pressure on their time or who found it more difficult to adjust to new ways. People also resent a feeling that they are being elbowed aside after a long period of unpaid service to the community. The formal complaint was that more centralised decision-making, especially when combined with more delegation to officials, was undemocratic. Those chosen by the electors had a public duty to ensure the efficient operation of local government, a responsibility that could not be carried out if councillors were barred from consideration of details. Such a view was most common amongst members of the smallest authorities where detailed control had been more practicable. But these councils were now going out of existence. This approach was also more typical of the 'backbench' councillor who was less likely to be nominated to represent his authority on the joint committees preparing for re-organisation. In the event there was little evidence that the joint committees had been affected by the fundamentalist democratic objections to Bains.

Yet the detailed acceptance of Bains may well have been an uncritical acceptance. Many joint committees adopted the model line by line, word by word, for example in relation to the terms of reference for a Policy and Resources Committee or the job specification for a Chief Executive. How many elected representatives who agreed to recommend that the Policy and Resources Committee should 'guide the Council in the formulation of its corporate plan of objectives and priorities' had given careful thought to this concept? But to follow Bains was the easy but responsible way out of a problem. The joint committees were weak bodies. They were transient. They were divided by institutional loyalties and often by political affiliations. They had no staff of their own. They had little time to prepare a management scheme for the new councils. The combination of urgency, lack of resources and the lack of corporate spirit created heavy pressure to agree to the centrally inspired solution.

Yet some joint committees, as noted above, did exercise independent judgement. Where Bains conflicted substantially with local attitudes the result was a modification of the model. So the joint committee proposals on management retained an element of variety. Indeed this itself was in accord with the text of the Bains Report: 'there is no one perfect system of management in local government any more than in any other sphere of activity'. The political element of local government also tended to produce diversity. Since the Bains working group consisted with one exception (a company secretary from ICI) of local government officials, it tended to neglect, quite properly, the political implications of its proposals. Where the party element on a joint committee was strong the dominant political group could determine the proposals to be presented to the new authority. And party activity can introduce further variations into the working of formal structures even where, on paper, they are similar.

How great was the influence of the joint committees on the management structures of the new councils? Inevitably, it was considerable. In many areas the leading members of the joint committee became the leading members of the new council. Where a party dominated a joint committee it usually also controlled the new authority. The newly elected councils had to move rapidly ahead to appoint chief officials and frame committee structures in order to be ready for the takeover on 1 April 1974. So novice councillors elected in 1973 had no experience and little time with which to challenge the advice bequeathed to them, even were they so inclined. In sum, the pressures on the new councils to follow joint committee recommendations were similar to those which constrained many joint committees to follow Bains. There were, however, many cases where the new authorities did not accept part of the plans prepared for them. Three factors contributed to these adjustments—a change in local party control, the appointment of a Chief Executive fresh to the area, and pressure from councillors for a more extensive role in committee work. The third factor led either to the creation of more committees or to a tendency to increase the size of committees. Yet it should be stressed that these changes were of secondary importance. The framework within which the new authorities set to work was essentially that devised by the preparatory joint committees and their associated working parties.

Finally, the question must be asked: should the new authorities have had their business pre-planned for them to such an extent? Should the new councillors not have been given a free hand to put their own ideas into practice? If so much is done in anticipation of elections, does this not make democracy a farce? There are many answers to this challenge. Had no preliminary work been done before the elections, then the new authorities would have needed a longer period before they were ready to become executive bodies. A longer overlap between the old and the new councils would have been confusing to the public, even more unsettling for staff and generally would have caused dislocation and delay in the development of local authority policies. Sudden change is inimical to the smooth running of administrative systems. It cannot be argued that the preparatory work was an assault on the democratic rights of new councils for they were fully entitled to reject any or all of the advice tendered to them. Criticism of the pre-planning also implies that the members of the new authorities might reasonably be expected to bring to local government not only fresh faces but fresh ideas superior to past wisdom. Such an idea is unrealistic. Yet here is a paradox. Normally, the claim that one should rely on past wisdom is a deeply conservative attitude which upholds the value of experience. In this instance the advice presented to the new councils was based on ideas of recent growth. Councillors elected in 1973 found themselves under pressure from their predecessors not to follow the ways of their predecessors.

NOTES

1. The original proposal was to hold county elections in April and district elections in November. The timetable was dropped because it clearly allowed inadequate time for the districts to make essential preparations.
2. A study of a particular joint committee, Cheshire, has been made by Bruce Wood. No county is typical. Cheshire was unusual in that its preparatory work was exceptionally well organised largely due to the strong leadership of the Clerk. Also, although the county suffered substantial territorial change, the two county boroughs added to it were small and unlikely to disturb the established county hegemony. Cf. *The Scope for Local Initiative* (Martin Robertson, 1974) Ch. 6.
3. Detailed advice on the initial agenda was given in DOE Circular 50/73.
4. DOE Circular 68/72, para. 12.
5. *Report of the Reorganisation Joint Committee for South Tyneside*, Part I, p. 9.
6. *Report of the Reorganisation Sub-Committee* (Manchester City Council).
7. For further details of joint committee suggestions for future committee structures see Alan Norton and J. D. Stewart, 'Recommendations to the New Local Authorities, 1973' in *Local Government Studies* No. 6, pp. 3–9.
8. *The New Local Authorities Management and Structure* (HMSO, 1972), Appendix J, p. 165.
9. Staff recruitment areas are discussed more fully in Ch. 6 *infra*.
10. See Staff Commission Circular 6/72, para. 9.
11. See p. 141 *infra*.

Chapter 3

CREATING THE NEW AUTHORITIES

The Varied Nature of the Problem
To get a public authority on to a working basis, four requirements
must be met. It needs legal powers, it needs finance, it needs staff
and it needs accommodation. The first two of these essentials were
provided, albeit inadequately, by the 1972 Act; the other two
demanded local action. But these requirements are the barest
minimum. For a public authority to work well, harmonious personal relations within the organisation must develop; there must be
good relations with other public bodies with allied responsibilities;
there must be a measure of public support and understanding.
Judged by these tests, the size of local problems varied greatly. At
one extreme were the authorities with unchanged boundaries and
little change in functions: the Isle of Wight County Council is an
obvious example. At the other extreme are the new authorities with
no inheritance and no tradition. The six metropolitan counties faced
the harshest struggle. They were a new breed of local authority
designed to work with, and sometimes to co-ordinate, district councils, most of which were based on former county boroughs
accustomed to local independence. So the metropolitan counties
were launched into an environment that was suspicious if not
actually hostile. They enjoyed little public understanding. Many of
the metropolitan county councillors had mixed feelings about the
new authority. They were divided not only by party loyalties but
also by geographical loyalties, the latter being less predictable and
therefore more important.

Local ties also influenced the non-metropolitan counties. Sentiment is a powerful force in local affairs. It was much easier to bring
together the separate parts of Lincolnshire and Suffolk, where reorganisation coincided with popular consciousness of the county
unit, than to join Herefordshire with Worcestershire which were
traditionally separate entities. Geographical factors also accentuate
divisions. The Malvern Hills separate Hereford and Worcester. But
the outstanding example is Humberside where the new county is

bisected by the River Humber—always seen as a natural barrier rather than a factor which unites. The decision that Grimsby and the northern part of the former Lindsey County Council area should be linked with the north bank was taken after the publication of Circular 8/71 which set out the initial boundary proposals of the Conservative Government. The concept of the new Humberside depends upon the building of the Humber Bridge which is not due for completion until 1977. Until then the county is heavily reliant upon an inconvenient and unreliable ferry service. No other authority has such a severe communications problem.

Authorities which suffered little change used the reorganisation as an opportunity to review their methods of management. There was some movement of staff to other employers; planning staff, in particular, were redistributed to correspond with the new distribution of planning functions. Some senior staff took the chance of early retirement. But the buildings remained. The sense of continuity was little disturbed.

For authorities without predecessors the situation over staff and buildings was a total contrast. There are three shire counties, Avon, Cleveland and Humberside, based on former county boroughs; the latter continued to exist as districts and so were entitled to retain the greater part of their administrative staff and buildings. These three shire counties, together with the six metropolitan counties, were in the worst position. However, West Yorkshire inherited some property as the general legatee[1] of the former West Riding County Council. Similarly Humberside enjoyed an inheritance from the old East Riding County Council, but this property at Beverley is of limited value since Humberside is much larger than was the East Riding and also because councillors from south of the Humber are unwilling to travel further north than Hull to attend meetings. Avon, Cleveland and the metropolitan counties other than West Yorkshire started without any 'general purpose' assets: all the property and staff transferred to them was related to a specific function, e.g. education or refuse disposal.

Thus the first and most urgent task was to acquire a physical home and to settle into it. These new councils had to take the best accommodation that was available. So they were often forced to acquire a lease on a modern commercial style office block, a dramatic contrast to the traditional shire hall or town hall. Avon has a sky-scraper block in the centre of Bristol. West Midlands County has the upper part of an Electricity Board building near the centre of Birmingham: at the end of March 1974 there was no external evidence of their occupation. Such buildings cannot be used for council meetings or any substantial public gathering. They lack any semblance of dignity. Some have open-plan offices, the advantages of which are a matter for debate.

Most of the new generation of authorities inherited the majority of their staff from their predecessors. As 1 April 1974 grew nearer more and more officials were working for both old and new councils. For many the changeover was gradual and smooth. A few senior appointments were made from outside the locality; in these cases the individual officer moved to his new post after working out three months' notice, or possibly his time was divided between old and new employees for a transitional period. But for an authority without predecessors there could be no evolution by easy stages. Old and new council business could not proceed side by side. The metropolitan counties and the three non-historic shires obtained a high proportion of administrative, professional and technical staff from other authorities in the neighbourhood. But naturally the outgoing authorities could not afford to lose a large number of staff months before the new system became operative as their own business still had to be carried on. Indeed, chief officers from these new authorities have told me that one of the early feelings in their new posts was one of loneliness. They were virtually on their own in large suites of offices with little furniture or equipment. A first task was to appoint deputies and other senior colleagues. Yet their colleagues, even when selected, had to stay with present employers for some time. So for some months the offices remained largely empty. There was relatively little work to do during the day but evenings were filled by telephone conversations with the new recruits making plans and arrangements for the future. Again there were great variations. The Greater Manchester County got off to an easier start than other authorities of its type as almost all its chief officers were recruited from the City of Manchester and so constituted a ready-made team.

The metropolitan counties and the non-historic shires also had a bigger problem in recruiting an adequate number of good quality staff. Some officers were attracted to the challenge of a pioneering venture; others preferred the stability of local authorities with roots firmly in the past. These nine authorities also had to spend large sums to get themselves established. Charges were incurred for rent, equipment, telephone installations and furnishing on a scale unknown to other local councils which could launch themselves from an established foundation. The Local Government Act 1972 allowed the 'shadow' councils the product of the rate of $\frac{1}{4}$p to cover costs before 1 April 1974. For councils like Avon the $\frac{1}{4}$p was hopelessly inadequate. Money had to be borrowed at the current very high rates of interest, thus adding to the costs of reorganisation. The rate support grant formula contained no provision to offset this exceptional burden.

Between the extremes of Avon and the Isle of Wight came the authorities with a medium amount of difficulty. The typical situation was a merger of two or three authorities or parts thereof. This required the creation of a unified staff structure, reallocation of accommodation and the harmonising of diverse policies and administrative methods. In terms of possession of resources, the position was very favourable as compared with authorities deprived of any automatic inheritance. In terms of personal relations and political (not necessarily party political) pressure, the problems could be more delicate. There was a danger of separate loyalties and mutual jealousies based on the former authorities among both staff and councillors. Evidence of such tension among councillors can be seen in arguments about where meetings should be held or where administrative headquarters should be sited. Where an authority had a natural administrative centre this type of controversy could be more readily avoided. Friction among staff was more private but it is idle to deny that there was some jockeying for position. Officers from the larger of the merging authorities were normally better qualified or more experienced than their colleagues from the smaller authorities. Accordingly one might properly expect them to be favoured when competing claims for promotion were assessed. But their advancement could lead to initial resentment among the staff from smaller councils.

In metropolitan areas there were added complications. Twenty-nine out of thirty-six metropolitan districts were based on a former county borough. Four contained two such authorities. Here the county borough element in the new district had to adjust to working within a two-tier system. There was concern at how far the new metropolitan county would seek to change established local policies, e.g. free car parking at Dudley. The remaining three metropolitan districts, Knowsley, Tameside and Trafford had the greatest immediate problem since they had no county borough organisation on which to build and so had to create wholly new education and social service departments. Yet these areas may well benefit from the challenge involved in building a new system. My impression is that staff morale was often highest in places where a wholly new system had to be created.

The general effect of reorganisation was, of course, to produce fewer and larger authorities with greater resources which opened up a prospect of wider horizons and optimism about future progress. Yet a few county authorities became smaller. They were faced with the financial and psychological burdens of contraction. The table below shows the counties which suffered a serious loss of population; cases of trivial loss, below three per cent, have been excluded.

POPULATION LOSS BY SHIRE COUNTIES

Shire	Before reorganisation (000s)	After reorganisation (000s)	Percentage fall
Lancashire	2,535	1,341	47·1
Northumberland	508	280	44·9
Somerset	608	387	36·3
Warwickshire	639	456	28·7
Durham	822	608	26·0
Cheshire	1,130	865	23·4
Gloucestershire	571	463	18·9
Buckinghamshire	598	476	16·2

The reduction of Lancashire was the most severe both proportionately and in absolute terms. But as Lancashire remains one of the largest shire counties perhaps the consequences were not so serious as those in Northumberland and Somerset. Where an authority contracts it is quite impossible to cut down its overhead costs and expenditure on staff *pro rata* with the reduction in population. A county that loses a third of its population cannot abandon a third of its shire hall. Nor will it operate with two-thirds of each chief officer. Warwickshire provides a typical illustration. It lost 28 per cent of its population but the reduction in staff was only 19 per cent. As the fall in teaching staff was proportionate to the drop in population, it follows that the reduction in administrative, professional, clerical and other grades of staff was less—nearer 13 per cent. Somerset is a more extreme case: with a population fall of 36 per cent the drop in staff was lower than in Warwickshire. It is true that Somerset provided some services for Avon on an agency basis but this is not an explanation of the disproportion. The truth is that local government is highly protective. Chief officers sought to protect their staff by proposing more generous staffing establishments. Councillors did not wish to force redundancies and were content to think in terms of better standards of service. So authorities which were cut down in size managed to avoid severe problems of redundancy. Some of their staff were happy to move away to authorities which were expanding and so offered better prospects. Others chose to retire early. Natural wastage also helped to ease the problem. These factors, combined with generous staffing standards, meant that few individuals were adversely affected.

There were, however, problems about morale and quality. As the more able and ambitious officers move on they leave behind the less adventurous, the second-class or those who are content to stay put until retirement. The sense of decline in Somerset must be less invigorating than the need to improvise in Avon. An aggravating factor in Warwickshire must be the inconvenient shape of the new county which opens the possibility that it may be further revised by the Boundary Commission. It is impossible to tell whether further change would make Warwickshire bigger, smaller or would eliminate it altogether.

Shires which have grown in size cannot be analysed in the same way as those which have contracted. Where two or more authorities are merged together, possibly with parts of other authorities added as well, the basis for a comparison between old and new councils does not readily exist. Metropolitan counties as a new type of local government organisation obviously defy close comparison with their forebears. Shire counties have grown largely from the absorption of county boroughs and these forced marriages necessarily produced tension. The degree of difficulty caused was affected by the balance of local political allegiance, the size of the borough(s) brought into a county and their location. Where shire headquarters are located in a former county borough, the problems of communication and accommodation are reduced. Leicester and Nottingham fall into this category. Where the places to be absorbed are set apart from the shire capital and also form a substantial proportion of the new county, as in Devon, East Sussex and Hampshire, there must be problems about how far and how soon the new county organisation can be centralised. Lewes, the traditional assize town and county centre for East Sussex, is a very small place from which to administer a county serving 650,000 people. Where large towns have been merged into a county and are distant from the county headquarters, there is a need, politically and administratively, for some element of decentralised administration. This problem is discussed in the chapter on county/district relationships.

The Shadow Councils—Politics and Organisation for the Future
Newly elected councillors to the shadow authorities were expected to take major decisions rapidly. The earliest council and committee

meetings of the new bodies established a system that may last for years. All this had to be done in a period when councillors were finding their feet in a new situation. Many did not know each other. The extent of personal acquaintance depended on how far former councillors had been re-elected, how far boundaries had changed and how far they had met previously, usually through political channels. Previous acquaintance was least where a council was formed from an amalgam of several authorities and there was a minimum of political organisation.

The early work of the new bodies was also untypical. It was not concerned with the usual problems of an on-going organisation, for the shadow authorities had no responsibility for current services. Their task was to plan and prepare. They had to arrange committee and departmental structures, allocate accommodation, agree a system of management, adopt standing orders, appoint chief officers and the most senior supporting staff, and accept schedules of staff establishments. Much of this activity had an abstract, even academic flavour. And many of the biggest issues had to be settled first, within weeks rather than months of the election.

It was inevitable that mistakes were made in such circumstances. At one metropolitan district, which shall be nameless, the newly elected majority party group held a private meeting to decide a committee structure for the new council and to choose chairmen. The meeting had before it a paper prepared by officers making suggestions; unfortunately the paper was concerned with departmental organisation not committee structure. The mistake was not discovered until after the meeting. By then it was too late to reverse what had been done. None of the embryo committee chairmen were prepared to surrender their newly achieved status. So the authority carries on with a committee for nearly every department. Some committees have so little to do that they are forced to discuss trivia. The waste of resources in terms of officers' time and members' time and allowances is not inconsiderable.

Party activity in the new councils was much greater than in their predecessors. Throughout this century the party element in local government has been spreading, especially in urban areas. Reorganisation accentuated this trend, for the rival political organisations were keen to control the new and larger authorities while many aldermen and older councillors, used to the less political ways, dropped out of public life. The change was noticed mainly in the shires, some of which started to operate through a party system for the first time. Formal recognition was given to party groups and party leaders. Committee places were allocated on the basis of so many to each group. Private meetings were held to decide local party policy: occasionally, as in Berkshire, these are treated as formal council sub-committees and are staffed by officials. County boroughs had worked on a political basis for decades but for many chief officers in the shires it involved a fresh way of doing business. Nowhere was the development of political organisation more fully discussed than in Nottinghamshire. In its local election manifesto entitled *The Way Ahead* the Nottinghamshire Labour Party argued that councillors needed full-time professional advice not bound by the strict code of political impartiality which governs local authority officers. After the Labour victory in Nottinghamshire its leader, Councillor Wilson, attempted to establish a Political Office to support members of his majority group by helping to develop party policy in practical terms, to monitor its achievements and to help to initiate future policies. It was argued that, in relation to policy-making, Labour needed help from highly qualified people who were positively sympathetic to the Party's attitudes. The original proposal was that the Political Office should be staffed partly by outsiders appointed on a political basis on short non-renewable contracts. It was stressed that the Political Office would have no power to take decisions or to supervise the work of county council staff: its only powers would be to call for information and have the chance of discussing policy issues with the permanent staff. The scheme was a logical development from the idea that Cabinet ministers need political assistants to supplement the advice of civil servants. Indeed, it is also analogous to the Central Policy Review Staff initiated to assist the Conservative Cabinet in 1970.

The idea for a Political Office met with widespread criticism. Some Labour councillors were uneasy about the scheme and the Conservative minority on the County Council opposed it. NALGO also objected because it felt it would confuse the public by blurring the image of impartiality now enjoyed by local authority staff. Further, there were doubts about how far the influence of the Political Office would extend or even whether it might become a type of spying organisation. So under pressure the original proposal was weakened. The Political Office became a Special Research Officer, a single temporary political appointment, who would assist the Labour leader and the other committee chairmen. Similar assistance was to be offered to the Conservative opposition. However, even this modified proposal was not acceptable to the Labour group on the Nottinghamshire Council. Finally it was agreed to appoint a personal assistant to committee chairmen who should be a serving local government officer and not be a political nomination.

The Nottinghamshire example is instructive for it shows that there is powerful resistance, both in terms of public opinion and professional opinion, to the development of party political bureaucracies in local councils. It can, of course, be argued that such opinion is misguided, that the effect is to weaken the position of councillors who lack the time, information and expertise to plan for the future in terms of the philosophy they present for the electorate's approval. Probably this issue will emerge again in the future.

Nottinghamshire and many other authorities have started to provide some secretarial services for councillors. The extent of the provision varies. It may simply cover typing or extend to arranging appointments and meetings for committee chairmen or political groups.

The balance of party forces had an important effect on getting the new authorities into working order. Naturally their policies were affected by whether the councillors were predominantly Conservative, Labour or Liberal. Even more important for the purpose of the smooth establishment of a new organisation was whether any political group had a majority. Where a council is firmly organised on party lines, a majority group can take decisions in the certain knowledge that they will be ratified at a formal council meeting. If the group has the will to provide coherent leadership, the council will follow. Opposition at council and committee meetings may still be strong and argumentative but the new institution can evolve with some sense of stability. A similar situation can exist where non-party councillors are generally content to accept the recommendations of a central Policy and Resources Committee. In a number of shire counties there was no dominant political group but the organisation developed smoothly, or fairly smoothly, on the basis of regular co-operation between Conservatives and Independents. But where a council had no political majority, with possibly three party groups plus some unpredictable independents, the task of making vital decisions could be slowed down by the need for unofficial negotiations to achieve compromise. In Warwickshire the first two meetings of the Steering Committee appointed to make basic recommendations on the new county organisation could not even agree on the election of a chairman. This was the result of a very close political balance. However the new councillors accepted fairly quickly that there was a limit to the extent to which decisions could be affected by the absence of one or two members. The worst case of confusion caused by a lack of effective leadership from councillors was in a non-metropolitan district: at Adur in Sussex four Chief Executives resigned in succession during 1973.

The party factor could also aggravate the situation in any area where the two tiers of principal authorities were opposed to each other politically. Such tension was most significant in the case of larger districts, notably the metropolitan districts. The 1973 elections produced Labour majorities in all the metropolitan counties. In South Yorkshire and Tyne and Wear the districts were also solidly Labour. Elsewhere, as shown in the table, ten metropolitan districts were anti-Labour. At Leeds, Labour formed the largest group but did not have a majority. The Liberals were in a similar position at Liverpool. Conservatives were the largest group in the other eight authorities and in some places had overall control. Bristol, the largest non-metropolitan district, was controlled by Labour but faced a Conservative majority on the Avon County Council.

PARTY CONFLICT IN METROPOLITAN AREAS

Labour metropolitan county	Non-labour metropolitan district
Greater Manchester	Bolton
	Bury
	Stockport
	Trafford
Merseyside	Liverpool
	Sefton
	Wirral
West Midlands	Solihull
West Yorkshire	Bradford
	Leeds

Even where the two tiers were in political harmony, there was often substantial conflict between them, especially in some metropolitan areas. One has the impression that some metropolitan counties tried to assert themselves unduly in order to try to prove that they were the senior partner in the new system. Often there is no clear party view on the type of issue involved in a county/district conflict. Councillors may face a conflict of loyalty but their sympathies tend to be drawn towards the authority on which they serve. The effect of joint membership of district and county councils is discussed below.[2]

Opinion within an authority can also be divided by geographical loyalties. County councillors representing former county boroughs often see problems a little differently from their political associates representing rural areas. Such a situation produces strains within a party group that party loyalty cannot always overcome.

Where the two tiers were opposed politically there was an extra incentive for disputes about agency, concurrent powers, transfer of property and the appointment and remuneration of staff. Examples will be found in later sections of this book. Yet the amount of strife must not be exaggerated. So long as discussions were conducted between officials there was strong pressure to reach compromise. The burden of work caused by the timetable of reorganisation was severe. Prolonged disputes added to the load. So the easy way forward was to reach agreements.

The novelty of the situation created conditions in which, as argued above, the advice of the preparatory joint committees was often persuasive. However, there was some resistance among the new councils to Bains-style streamlined management. As the shadow authorities developed their organisational structure, the number of committees and sub-committees tended to increase. Councillors wanted to be given more to do. It is arguable that the numbers of councillors are too great, especially in metropolitan counties. The latter are concerned with strategic planning in its broadest aspects which arguably requires less intense local representation than the administration of personal services. The table below shows that the number of elected representatives in metropolitan counties is not determined by population nor by population density. South Yorkshire has a relative sparsity of population which may produce a reasonable claim for more councillors; in Tyne and Wear no such case can be made.

COUNCILLOR–POPULATION RATIO IN METROPOLITAN COUNTIES

County	Population (000s)	Councillors	People per hectare	Councillor population ratio*
Greater Manchester	2,730	106	21	1:25,700
Merseyside	1,621	99	25	1:16,400
South Yorkshire	1,319	100	8	1:13,200
Tyne and Wear	1,198	104	22	1:11,500
West Midlands	2,785	104	31	1:26,800
West Yorkshire	2,080	88	10	1:23,600

* Correct to three significant figures.

The following miscellany of examples shows other aspects of the retreat from Bains. Leicestershire and Nottinghamshire have separate committees for Policy and Resources. At Dudley the four sub-committees of the Policy and Resources Committee as recommended by Bains were upgraded to become full committees of the Council and report to both the Policy and Resources Committee and the full Council. Surrey took a similar view. Wakefield does not have a Policy and Resources Committee. The new Northamptonshire Council dropped the proposal for a Performance Review Subcommittee. In Somerset the Joint Committee plan for a joint county/district planning service broke down.[3] In the few areas where the joint committees had not been very effective, their influence was necessarily reduced. The Staffordshire Joint Committee had avoided making decisions owing to uncertainty about the political balance on the new county council. Similarly, the West Midlands Joint Committee failed to produce firm ideas for a committee structure and the newly elected metropolitan council moved away from Bains by appointing a Finance Committee separate from the Policy and Resources Committee.

The framing of standing orders raised a variety of issues which can be said to affect the democratic element of local council business. Labour councillors commonly favour afternoon or evening meetings which make it easier for wage earners to attend. Conservatives generally prefer meetings to start mid-morning. Another related item was frequency of meetings: Labour councillors felt that a quarterly cycle in the shire tradition was inadequate. There are other issues which affect the rules of debate at council meetings. Some authorities still retain a clause in standing orders which permits a committee chairman to refuse to answer a question on the agenda paper. Alternatively, supplementary questions may not be permitted. Motions on the agenda of the council may be referred to the appropriate committee without the possibility of debate. Shadow authorities also had to decide how far their deliberations should be public. Section 100 of the 1972 Act gives the press and public a right of admission to committees unless a committee decides that a particular item should be dealt with *in camera*. But this section did not become law until 1 April 1974 so the shadow authorities could agree to evade publicity. This section also raises the permanent question of how far delicate items will be shunted to sub-committees to avert intrusion by the public. There is no requirement to provide access to sub-committees and few authorities, with Bedfordshire and Berkshire among the exceptions, permit the press to attend them.

An immediate task of the shadow authorities was to appoint their chief officers. The first appointment to be made was that of Chief Executive. At least in theory, this raised a dual problem—what sort of qualifications were desirable as well as who to choose. The idea that the Chief Executive should have overall charge of administration and be spared the day-to-day toil or responsibility for a department implied that legal qualifications were not necessary.[4] Indeed no specific qualifications were needed. The field was wide open for selection committees to choose who they felt to be the best administrator available. Chief Executives for the counties and the metropolitan districts could be recruited from anywhere in England and Wales except local authorities in London.[5] Many treasurers, planners, educationalists and engineers did apply for chief executive posts. Almost none was successful. The selection committees were cautious: they relied on lawyers and usually preferred local candidates. In twenty-five shires the new Chief Executives were the Clerks or Deputy Clerks of the former county or, where there was an amalgamation of top-tier authorities, of the largest partner in the amalgamation. Three shires chose the Clerk of one of its smaller constituent authorities, i.e. the Town Clerks of Leicester, Oxford and York. Nine shires chose outsiders who were Clerks or Deputy Clerks of local authorities elsewhere. The two remaining shires showed a little greater initiative. Cleveland appointed the Treasurer of Teesside. Somerset, where the selection was delayed, was the sole case of an appointment from outside local government.[6] Three of the metropolitan counties chose the Clerk of the largest authority within their own boundaries. Tyne and Wear selected the Town Clerk of Sunderland which missed being the largest authority in the area by a few thousand souls. South Yorkshire appointed the Deputy Clerk of the West Riding. West Midlands nominated the Town Clerk of Coventry who had previously been the Treasurer of that City. Metropolitan districts, with few exceptions, followed the pattern of appointing a local Clerk. However, untypical choices were made at Birmingham (the Chief Planner of Liverpool) and Doncaster (the Treasurer of the Doncaster Rural District).

The selection of other chief officers provides fewer items of interest. The choice was restricted to local applicants unless the Local Government Staff Commission had given permission for a national advertisement.[7] Also there was less scope for argument, except perhaps in the case of Directors of Social Services, about the type of professional qualifications required. Royston Greenwood has shown that the number of 'outside' chief officer appointments to the top-tier authorities was limited although it was a little higher in the case of Directors of Education and Social Services in the metropolitan districts.[8]

Speedy decisions were important. A new organisation cannot be built up satisfactorily until executive heads have been chosen and are available to take up their duties at least on a part-time basis. The need for rapid action was widely understood and almost everywhere top appointments were quickly made. Speed reduced uncertainty and was good for staff morale. Authorities which were first off the mark had the strongest field of candidates. Competitive interviews were arranged to ensure that justice was seen to be done even where the outcome was a foregone conclusion.[9] Hampshire was a notable exception in this general scene of rapid action. Here none of the candidates on the short list for Chief Executive proved acceptable to the appointing committee. So the post was readvertised and there was unfortunate delay before it was filled. As a result other senior appointments and preparations for the new structure were slowed down. In both Durham and Somerset the Clerks of the outgoing County Councils accepted the posts of Chief Executive to the new counties and then changed their minds and decided to retire. The newly appointed Chief Executive at Newcastle resigned after a few months owing to ill-health. Another newly appointed Chief Executive, formerly responsible for technical services, resigned after a few months when he found that purely administrative duties were uncongenial. There were other cases where chief officers delayed their decision to retire and subsequently departed. Some newly appointed senior officers later accepted similar posts with larger authorities and which, therefore, were better paid. My impression is that this pattern was more common in the Midlands and the North, than in the South of England, due to the presence of the metropolitan counties. It is quite impossible to freeze the movement of local government staff completely, even for a short period. But due to the efforts of the Local Government Staff Commission the disruption caused by staff changes was less serious than it might have been.[10]

Some of the shadow authorities failed to gain full co-operation from the outgoing councils. Dying or diminished institutions can be petty. They may try to protect purely local interests and ignore wider considerations. One example was attempts made to influence the future use and ownership of property.[11] And one county borough, a few days before its demise, placed a conservation order on a site where the new metropolitan district intended to build urgently required office accommodation. Whether the order was justified on environmental grounds must be a matter of opinion: on any view, the incident is scarcely an indication of goodwill between the old and new authorities.

Administrative and Financial Preparations

For reorganisation to work smoothly it was vital that the methods to be followed should be worked out well in advance. On all major questions and some minor aspects of reorganisation, local authorities were guided by Circulars of advice from central departments. This gave the advantage of some uniformity of treatment. However, at national level the preparations fell rather behind schedule. An initial reason was that the Local Government Bill took rather longer to pass through Parliament than had been anticipated. *Inter alia,* this had the effect of delaying the establishment of joint committees for the metropolitan districts, and some rushing of consultation procedures. An example of haste was the issue of a Consultative Document[12] to local authority associations on 2 February 1973 which asked for comments in three weeks on the draft Commencement Orders: the purpose of these Orders was to bring parts of the 1972 Act into effect before the changeover date so that shadow councils would have legal authority to start work as soon as they had been elected. The reorganisation timetable also fell behind schedule in relation to agency and transfer of property and staff. To an extent these delays were cumulative. Agency caused more local difficulties than had been anticipated. And the rate of the new attendance allowance for councillors was not announced until December 1973 whereas the original intention had been that the scale of the allowance should be made known before people decided to offer themselves for election to the new councils. Indeed, Circular 16/74 which set out the conditions under which allowances could be paid did not appear until February 1974: even then some questions concerning taxation and social security benefits in relation to the allowance had not been finally settled.

The process of bringing the 1972 Act into effect by stages was one of some complexity. Provisions relating to the areas and constitution of the new authorities came into effect as soon as the Bill had reached the Statute Book. So also did the sections authorising the planning of and early preparations for the new' system, including transitional arrangements for the discharge of functions, the initial expenses of new councils and schemes for new combined police forces. Other legal changes required at once could be described as tidying-up operations: as the 1972 Act ended the delegation of powers by local education authorities there was no sense in retaining a moment longer the section of the Local Government Act 1958 which permitted districts to apply for delegated powers. Other parts of the 1972 Act to take immediate effect had no necessary connection with reorganisation, e.g. the declaration by officers of their interest in contracts, the termination of ministerial control over local authority ferry charges and wider powers to deal with emergencies and disasters.

The second stage of the legal process was a Statutory Instrument which applied certain sections of the 1972 Act to the new councils.[13] This Order became operative in the case of the counties the day after their election, for metropolitan districts two days after the election and for non-metropolitan districts four days after. The sections then activated were concerned with the tasks of the shadow councils in the changeover period before they took over full executive responsibility. Thus they were given powers to appoint committees, appoint staff, acquire land, accept property, make contracts, undertake research, provide information, insure councillors while on council business and pay subscriptions to associations of local authorities. They were required to establish a general rate fund and assume responsibility for their own financial administration. They were authorised to spend money on concurrent functions and make provision for the custody of documents. Their minutes and accounts had to be available for public inspection. The new authorities were also given a general power to take necessary interim action in relation to the functions they were to inherit on 1 April 1974.

This same day saw the third and main stage of the implementation of the 1972 Act when the new councils took over the actual operation of services. Yet this was still not the end of the process, for other 'clearing up' exercises are still to come. Arrangements for the appointment of local valuation panels to hear appeals against rate assessments are due to be revised under paragraph 29 of the thirteenth Schedule to the 1972 Act. These new schemes are not expected to be ratified before 1976. It will take even longer to deal with the jungle of local legislation. But the intention of Section 262 is to force a drastic simplification in this area. All existing local Acts relating to metropolitan counties will be repealed in 1979; those relating to shire counties will go in 1984. In the meantime councils are to consider how far these local laws are essential and to prepare fresh legislation to continue any provisions that are still needed. The need for local legislation will be curtailed by a Government Bill conferring generally on councils those local Act powers which experience has shown to be useful.

Reshaping of local boundaries creates an immediate problem in relation to local legislation. Either the areas to which local Acts relate must be changed or local powers must be applied in accordance with their original geographical limitations. The first course requires alteration of statute law: the second does not. In the interest of simplicity the second alternative was chosen. The result is that local authorities now have to operate local legislation on a patchwork basis because a local Act may well not apply to the whole area of an authority but only to those places subject to the particular Act before 1 April 1974. Where this situation presented intolerable difficulties, the Government agreed to make a Provisional Order to amend the spatial application of a local law. These Orders required ratification by a Provisional Order Confirmation Bill; however, this Bill could not have been prepared in time for passage through the 1973–4 session of Parliament, irrespective of the general election.

The establishment of new authorities raised a myriad of issues that required decision. Should old methods of administration be retained? Often authorities which were merged to form a new unit had previously used different systems: a choice had now to be made between alternatives. Each detail, although of limited significance in itself, could create trouble if not given adequate forethought. Matters which appeared to be trivial may come to have policy implications. The vast majority of the items listed below were settled by senior officials rather than councillors, although formal ratification by the latter was sometimes required.

Accommodation was a major problem in many areas. A local authority must have a physical home. Reference has been made already to the unequal inheritance enjoyed by the new councils. But often the problem was not so much a lack of available space; the trouble arose from the nature and distribution of the premises. A metropolitan district formed from nine small boroughs and urban districts had nine council chambers, but no building was large enough to bring together its main departments. Many authorities have dispersed offices with consequent problems of communication which even modern aids like telex do not overcome. It is an unhappy paradox that Bains-style attempts to diminish departmentalism through the concept of corporate management should have coincided with greater physical separation of local authority departments. Some authorities gained advantage from the slump in the commercial property market and were able to lease large office blocks. The social services department of a metropolitan district is situated in a new shopping precinct in a building designed to be a bowling alley. Other councils were not so fortunate. Office reorganisation involves also much detailed work in relation to furnishings, equipment, telephones, etc. There was also a need to give the public full information about the relocation of offices. Many shadow authorities made a great effort to explain the new situation to the public through press publicity.

One of the first tasks of the new authorities was to appoint a 'proper officer' for various purposes. To increase flexibility in administration the 1972 Act reduced statutory controls over the appointment of senior local government officers and the allocation of duties to particular office-holders. But it was still necessary for an identifiable individual to be charged with certain responsibilities defined by law, e.g. electoral registration officers and officers deputed to receive declarations of interest by councillors. Such nominations are now a matter for local decision. A council has to pass a resolution that the occupant of a specified office on its staff shall be the 'proper officer' for a particular purpose. In practice these duties are largely divided between the Chief Executive, the Secretary and the Treasurer, but the actual distribution varies from authority to authority.

The transfer from old authorities to the new created many problems of financial administration.[14] Initial expenses of the new 'shadow' authorities were covered by funds obtained from the outgoing councils which levied a rate of one-quarter of a new penny to provide revenue for their successors. This amounted to a total additional rate of half a new penny, divided equally between the new county and the new district authorities. Payment was to be made within fourteen days of the first meeting of a new council or such later date as might be agreed locally. Where a rating authority was divided between two or more new counties or districts its contribution was divided in accordance with the respective shares of the new bodies to the rate product. As noted above, these sums proved inadequate in some areas but the shadow authorities had power to borrow and so could meet their immediate commitments. For most of the new councils their initial expenses related largely to salaries of senior staff who were often appointed on a part-time basis and who divided their attention between old authorities and the new. Much of the recruitment was on a very local basis so the old and new employers often overlapped geographically. Thus the allocation of salary cost was very much a matter for local adjustment and was not of importance save where an officer moved outside the area of his former employer.

In many cases amalgamated authorities had used alternative forms of data processing—manual, computer-based, or mechanical but non-computer methods. Naturally, reorganisation further advanced the use of computers but the new authorities had to decide how far to use computer processes and what installations were needed to carry them out. This could be a matter of forward planning as it was sometimes necessary to use existing methods in existing offices after 1 April 1974 until a new and rationalised system could be launched.

Internal audit systems had to be harmonised and, at least in larger authorities, agreement had to be reached about their liaison with management services. There was a need to build up a working relationship with the external auditors who might also be changed as the new authorities were given a choice between district audit and approved professional auditors. In the event, most councils retained district audit. Among the counties only Nottinghamshire and Somerset chose professional audit while Tyne and Wear divided the job between professional and district audit. Twenty-nine metropolitan districts opted for district audit while Birmingham, Coventry and Gateshead opted for professional audit and Leeds, St Helens, Solihull and Stockport split the job. Over 90 per cent of non-metropolitan districts also chose district audit.

Each new authority required a set of financial regulations before 1 April 1974 to govern procedure for awarding contracts and the role of committees in relation to finance and budgeting. The form of revenue and capital estimates had to be agreed as a preliminary to producing rate estimates for the new authority. How far the shadow authorities were themselves able to take full charge of assembling the basis for the 1974 rate estimate varied from place to place. Where authorities were amalgamated the figures tended to emerge from bringing together material produced by the councils that were going out of existence subject, of course, to any changes of policy agreed by the shadow council.

Decisions had to be made about the use of accountancy systems which needed to adapt to the requirements of computerisation and the various financial and statistical returns required by central government. Some finance departments were also attempting to develop the concept of programme budgeting; this again had an effect on accountancy methods. An associated problem was the choice of a costing system which might have to include the control of a direct labour organisation.

Methods of raising capital also vary between authorities. Where authorities merged there might be a need to choose between alternative practices. With larger authorities the minimum size of sums borrowed is likely to increase and there is a stronger case for establishing a consolidated loans fund or mortgage pool. Some local authorities obtain part of their loan capital through marketable bonds but the Treasury places a restriction on the amount of an

C

authority's debt that may be obtained in this way. Because the ceiling is not expressed as a uniform percentage of total debt some new authorities found that through their inherited liabilities they had on issue bonds in excess of their entitlement. Where this occurred all existing bonds were unaffected but no more bonds could be issued or renewed until such action could be taken without exceeding the permitted maximum. Part I of Schedule 13 of the 1972 Act gave local authorities an additional means of meeting their capital requirements by allowing foreign borrowing subject to Treasury consent. Previously this power was available only through local legislation. In a letter to local authorities dated 21 March 1974 the Treasury intimated that foreign borrowing would be restricted to counties with a 'relevant loan debt' of £400 million or more. Counties were expected to form consortia with their districts and the relevant loan debt was the aggregate of the debt of the county and any district that joined the scheme. Where foreign borrowing was used it was actually undertaken by the county except in Merseyside and Greater Manchester where it was agreed that the work should be done by the highly experienced Treasurer's departments of the cities of Liverpool and Manchester.

The contractual liabilities of the outgoing authorities had to be reviewed. Reorganisation diminished the need for smaller, separate orders of goods and services. It was desirable that invoices for supplies delivered before 1 April 1974 should be obtained fairly rapidly so that the accounts of former authorities could be closed. The burden of closing accounts varied greatly, e.g. the new Lincolnshire had to clear up the financial affairs of three former counties. In the interests of simplicity there was a certain amount of rough justice in allocating charges between the old and the new authorities. For example, the general arrangement was that telephone accounts payable in March 1974 were settled by the old authorities while those payable in April were paid by the new authorities in spite of the fact that rentals are paid for in advance and calls in arrear. Decisions had to be made about the destruction of old records: alternatively, where records were preserved, the issue became one of where they should be kept. When a new local government unit was formed by amalgamation, the probability was that the former authorities had used separate banks and insurance companies. So there was a need to unify banking and insurance arrangements. Decisions were required about the use of pre-signed cheques and the countersigning of cheques in excess of a certain amount. A new authority could also be expected to review the amount of insurance cover it required, especially as money values were being eroded by inflation.

Of all the more routine aspects of reorganisation there is no doubt that the most critical was the care of the payroll. It was essential to ensure that on the first pay-day after 1 April 1974 those entitled to a wage, salary or pension were, in fact, paid. The task was relatively easy in the case of simple amalgamations, the main decision being whether to integrate payroll systems before, on or after the appointed day. The need to standardise pay periods, pay dates and pay methods could require consultation with trade unions. Where an authority was divided, the vital task was to ensure that no employee was 'lost' in the changeover and was not paid at all. Another possibility to guard against was that of someone being paid twice! In the event, there were some local difficulties. Some manual workers at Doncaster went on strike because their pay was said to be incorrect. A salary rise for teachers became payable on the changeover day and this added to the likelihood of mistakes. When things went awry there was a tendency for the new councils to blame the accuracy of the information received from the former employers. But there were also difficulties, not always sufficiently foreseen, in adjusting computerised information from one system to another. Resources available for planning and establishing new records were limited; the situation was aggravated in many places by the movement of middle management staff in finance departments which meant that some officers in charge of pay were unfamiliar with local conditions. In other aspects of administration a little extra delay is permissible while new situations are mastered. But pay must be available on pay day. Here the calendar is the complete autocrat. Mistakes which directly affect personal income are deeply resented. One county treasurer has commented that 'it is really quite extraordinary how vitriolic people can be in such circumstances'.

The need for care in relation to individual payments extends from local government staff to the general public. For many services local authorities make assessment of individual income in order to determine rates of charge or rates of grant. The functions concerned include education (remission of school meals charges, clothing grants, higher education grants), social services and rent rebates as well as rate rebates. The problems here related not simply to the need for the transfer of accurate information but also to the harmonisation of policies. Certainly there were issues about how far these assessments should be separate for each service or whether they should be unified. This question is particularly important in metropolitan districts; in the shires there is a division of responsibility between education and social services at county level and the district control of housing and rating so that the element of unification cannot be so complete. With the growth of means testing there are major administrative economies to be gained from the centralisation of this type of work. Centralisation can also ease the form filling required of the client or applicant. But there are obvious dangers here for individual privacy and it is important to control access to registers of personal detail. The accuracy of a central register also becomes of crucial importance because the effects of error are multiplied when information is used for several purposes.

Finally, the new authorities had to survey their assets and problems of income collection. Staff responsible for collecting fees and charges had to be made familiar with new banking procedures. Sometimes policy decisions were needed to equalise charges for similar services. The issues could vary from the trivial, e.g. fees for the use of tennis courts, to those of great importance, in particular council house rents. A survey of rate collection was required where diverse methods had formerly been used in different parts of a new authority's area. How far and how rapidly should variations be eliminated? How far should local offices be used for rent and rate collection? Policy decisions were needed on various aspects of rate collection where the practice of amalgamating authorities had diverged: this applied to such questions as whether to give rebate for prompt payment, whether to provide for payment by frequent instalments and whether to rate empty properties.

Many local trusts and bequests were transferred from the old authorities to the new. Here again the recipients wanted full information in advance, particularly in order to distinguish which trusts needed more active and continuous management. Reorganisation also involved the merging of loans pools and superannuation funds. Decisions had to be taken about the pattern of future investment in anticipation of accumulation of further resources. In some areas the position was complicated because the investment of superannuation funds was affected by local Acts. It was desirable also that new authorities should organise inventories of property inherited from their predecessors. The compilation of such a register could well raise questions as to whether particular items could be more profitably used or perhaps sold.

Transfer of Property
The transfer of property from the old authorities to the new was effected by Orders under Section 254 of the 1972 Act. These were issued after extensive discussion with the associations of local authorities. A consultation paper was followed in the summer of 1973 by a publication, *Local Government Reorganisation in England*.

Transfer of Property—Memorandum which set out the Government's 'firm conclusions'. A second edition of the Memorandum, a much longer booklet, appeared in December 1973, a month after the Statutory Instrument[15] that set out the general principles of transfer. This revised version incorporated some refinements of the rule system and covered additional topics, in particular the procedure for settling disputes. There followed supplementary Orders dealing with specific areas—the fire service, magistrates' courts, the probation service and joint boards abolished as from 1 April 1974.

It is common to think of property in terms of land and buildings but, of course, it covers equipment (including vehicles), records, stores, contractual rights, outstanding balances and loan debts. Property involves liabilities as well as assets. Disputes could arise not simply from the reallocation of assets but also from the distribution of liabilities.

Outstanding balances in rate funds and capital funds on 31 March 1974 were passed on to the new authorities. The new top-tier authorities inherited the assets of county councils; the second-tier inherited from the old county boroughs and county districts. Where a former authority was partitioned, then its liquid assets were divided among its successors in proportion to their shares of its rateable value. (Balances on housing revenue accounts were treated on a different basis: here the apportionment was made on the numbers of houses handed on to the new councils.) This scheme of distribution could work unfairly. If a new county based upon an amalgam of former authorities received substantial balances from some of its predecessors and little or nothing from the others, the ratepayers in the latter areas gained benefit at the expense of the others. County boroughs made no contribution at all to new counties. However, these were not major problems since the balances available for transfer were not large. One exception was Lancashire where substantial sums were paid to Greater Manchester and Merseyside; to achieve greater equity Greater Manchester agreed that 50 per cent of the money received from Lancashire should be redistributed to its districts proportionately to their share of the rateable value of the old Lancashire.

Transfer of tangible assets obeyed a simple principle. Property should follow the use to which it had been put. If property X had been used for function Y and if function Y had been transferred from authority A to authority B, then after 1 April 1974 X would belong to B. Unfortunately this formula did not cover a variety of situations. There were complications wherever a function or an area was divided. If property had been used for more than one purpose it was possible that not all these purposes were inherited by the same authority. Alternatively, where property had been used to provide a service, in particular a specialised service for a wide area, the area may have been divided by the new local boundaries. Besides these general problems, there were some more technical issues and some awkward questions arising from local circumstances.

The obvious solution in the case of a multi-purpose property was to determine which of the new authorities would use the greater part of it on the assumption that the existing use pattern continued. The measurement could be done in various ways but for buildings the occupation of floor space was the obvious yardstick. If no single function could claim 50 per cent occupation, the property went to the function with the biggest single claim unless this could be over-matched by a combination of functions adhering to an authority other than that responsible for the function with the largest use. The location of the property, whether inside or outside an authority's area, was not relevant for this purpose.

Where the area of a former authority was divided, a specific authority was designated as a legatee in the official Memorandum on the Transfer of Property. Where areas were not divided, there were 'general legatees': for a former county this, naturally, was the new county that included the old one; for former boroughs and districts it was the new district that included them. That county borough assets passed to the districts was especially hard on the new shire counties based on former county boroughs, e.g. Avon and Cleveland. The general legatees inherited property used for con-current functions—which were defined as excluding highways but including car parks. One result of this rule was that municipal aerodromes remained with the districts in default of a local agreement to the contrary. General legatees also acquired general purpose property not used mainly for a particular function: here the word 'mainly' was defined as applying where an authority other than the legatee could substantiate a claim that its functions were entitled to a 50 per cent use of the property.

Subject to the operation of the use criterion, which determined allocation between counties and districts, property in divided areas was transferred to the new authority in which it was situated. However, where a divided authority owned property outside its area, such property was inherited by its general legatee.

The general principles covered the vast majority of items quite adequately and showed unmistakably how transfers should be made. Yet there was a residue of problems. There might be argument about the purpose for which property had been used or was to be used. Temporary use was ignored. So if land acquired for central area redevelopment was a car park until building could start, the car park was irrelevant for purposes of transfer. Another possibility was that an outgoing council might seek to designate property in a way that would influence its future ownership. One example is that of a county borough which, just before reorganisation, purchased an expensive site for school playing fields which it proposed should replace existing playing fields. The latter were then designated as land for building council houses. Loan charges on the new playing fields would become a responsibility of the county as the local education authority while the new district, the former county borough, would get a housing site on the cheap. To prevent 'cheating' of this kind, designations of use made after 9 November 1973, the day on which the Statutory Instrument was issued, could be challenged under the disputes procedure. The Secretary of State also had a reserve power to over-rule unreasonable designations made before that date.

Other difficulties arose because the concept of 'a property' was nowhere defined. The common-sense view is that a building is a single property and cannot be split. But must a piece of land be a single property? If a local authority owns a site that is to be used partly for highway purposes and partly for housing, it is not unreasonable for a line to be drawn on a map to divide the land into two parcels. Provided this division had been formally recorded before 9 November 1973, the land was duly split between the new highway and housing authorities for the area.

Another problem related to buildings in the course of being replaced. Suppose that a county borough had a fire station adjacent to the town hall which was being replaced by a new fire station and that the site of the existing station was intended to allow expansion of the town hall. Under the normal rules of transfer the site would go to the county as the new fire authority and so would not be readily available to improve the town hall which probably had become the headquarters of the new district. An exception to the general rules allowed such property to be allocated on the basis of its future use, rather than existing use, providing two conditions were satisfied. The holding authority must have passed a formal resolution about its future use before 8 November 1973 and the site must be peculiarly suitable for the purpose so designated. Again, any disagreement arising from such action was settled under the disputes procedure.

Refuse disposal sites presented particular difficulties both because this function was moved from districts to counties and also because the use made of these sites is changed after tipping has been completed. A former tip can become a very pleasant public open space. The rule is that ownership depends on the future use of the site provided that the 'old' owner has passed a resolution before 9 November 1973 to determine what it should be.

Agency agreements did not affect the distribution of property. The council that has statutory responsibility for a function is entitled to property used for that function in accordance with the general rules described above, irrespective of any local arrangement that some other authority should carry out particular duties.

So far this discussion has concentrated on ownership. The general intention was that property should continue to be used for the same purposes after 1 April 1974 as heretofore. Any other plan would have created impossible accommodation problems on the handover day. So where an authority had a 'minority' claim on a building it could continue to occupy an appropriate share subject to meeting a due proportion of the expenses including any loan charges. This right applied whether a 'minority' situation arose from a division of function or a division of area. Thus the education and social services offices of a former county borough may stay in the town hall until the shire county decides to move them away. Another example relates to division of area: a children's home owned by a former county that has been split is now owned by the legatee authority, but the other new county having part of the area of the former owners is entitled to a share of the places in the home subject to paying an equivalent share of the cost. An authority with user rights can apply them to any of its functions. So a county with an education office in the town hall of a former county borough could decide to use the office to administer any other county activity. Had user rights been restricted to original purposes, there would have been a tendency to ossify the allocation of resources since rationalisation could have led to loss of rights. An authority that failed to exercise user rights could not claim compensation although it might negotiate some recompense. Where authorities were divided it is likely that their successors inherited rights outside their territory, e.g. South Yorkshire had rights in County Hall, Wakefield. Such rights were of little use, at least in the long term. Should compensation have been payable in such cases? The conflict here is between equity and simplicity. To have given a right to compensation would have led to complex and costly valuation disputes. However, if a council decides to sell a property in which another authority has rights, compensation is payable.

Contents of a building did not necessarily accompany the ownership of the building, for contents are divisible. Thus equipment, stores and records can normally be split up and this is a natural solution where the area of an authority is divided. However, some assets lose value if taken into separate parts. A computer in two pieces will not give satisfaction. It may be disadvantageous to parcel out a specialised library. Situations of this kind were settled by local agreements, usually involving joint use.

Where local authorities agreed that property should be transferred otherwise than in accord with the general rules, such property was listed as an exception to the provisions of the transfer order. Where there was no agreement, the disputes machinery came into effect. There were four possible bases for dispute. They were: issues of fact; issues on which agreement was essential, e.g. allocation of vehicles; special situations, e.g. appropriations after 9 November 1973 and replaced buildings; and issues involving interpretation of the law. Various issues of fact could arise, e.g. the purpose for which property had been held, whether or not its present use was temporary, the chief use of a property used for more than one purpose, whether tipping at a refuse dump had been completed. Legal arguments about the interpretation of the Order could be referred to the courts either instead of arbitration or after the arbitration procedure had been exhausted.

The disputes procedure operated under the terms of the Arbitration Act 1950. The authorities concerned could themselves organise the proceedings but if they failed to agree upon the choice of arbitrator then the Secretary of State made the nomination. Adjudication could be either by a single umpire or by a panel of three. The Government Memorandum commented that senior and possibly retired local government officers were suitable for the task but they should not have been connected with the area involved in the dispute. As disputes were not settled until after the changeover date, the property concerned stayed in the custody of the legatee authority until the arbitration decision had been given.

The vast majority of potential disputes were resolved by compromise or by withdrawal of a claim. So long as bargaining remained in the hands of officials, an acceptable formula was likely to emerge. Agreement was more difficult when elected representatives were drawn into negotiations, especially where contesting councils were opposed politically. At this stage a dispute easily becomes a question of prestige. It is also more difficult to secure agreement on subjects which readily arouse controversy and readily attract publicity. Agreement is also more difficult where authorities have competing claims to provide a service. Airports are a good example. Under the 1972 Act civic aerodromes are a concurrent function of counties and districts so, unless local agreements are made to the contrary, municipal airports remain district property. Nevertheless, the future of airports caused argument in many areas. Greater Manchester felt it had a reasonable claim to Ringway Airport since it was the transportation authority and would have to finance traffic improvements in the Manchester District, e.g. a possible tube railway. It was argued that profits from the airport should help to meet these costs. Finally it was agreed that the airport should be operated by a county/district joint committee with the profit or loss equally shared. Another example of a dispute that faded is the York Museum. Museums are another concurrent power. The one in York had been held by the City as an educational trust and under the 1972 Act, Section 210, educational trust property was to be transferred to the local education authority, i.e. North Yorkshire. The outgoing York City Council appealed to the Department of the Environment to make a special exception for their museum. The County raised no objection and the matter appeared to be settled when the newly elected York District Council decided that it wished the trust to pass to the County so that the museum could be paid for out of the county rate rather than the district rate. Another case where there can be doubt as to which authority administers property is extra-territorial council housing. After some hesitation Liverpool decided that its estates outside the City boundaries should be handed over to the districts in which they were situated.

The transfer of property rules were designed to be fair, to be as simple as possible and to minimise opportunities for dispute. Inevitably, these desiderata conflicted. The second edition of the Memorandum on Transfer was longer and more complex than the original: simplicity had to retreat to allow greater fairness. It is arguable that the rules are unduly favourable to districts which include former county boroughs, for the county inherits no county borough property save that directly used for what have become county responsibilities. An even stronger case can be made to show that the three metropolitan districts that do not include a former county borough have been treated badly. Here the districts suffer and the counties gain as the second-tier authorities often have no rights to ownership of specialised facilities for education to which local ratepayers have contributed in the past. Any attempt to have met these difficulties would have made the rules of transfer even more intricate. Greater complexity would have created more administrative difficulties and disputes; it would also have opened the way to fresh claims of unfairness.

NOTES

1. For an explanation of this concept, see p. 70.
2. See p. 76 *infra.*
3. See pp. 86-7 *infra.*
4. Before 1974 there had been a few isolated cases of the appointment of a non-lawyer to be the top administrator of a local authority, but the Bains recommendations about the functions of chief executives greatly increased the prospect that non-lawyers might be chosen.
5. See p. 132 *infra.*
6. Mr Maurice Gaffney, the Somerset Chief Executive appointed in October 1973, had been previously the General Manager of the Telephone Manufacturing Company, a restaurateur and the Chief Executive of the West Hertfordshire Main Drainage Authority. He had also been a GLC committee chairman and had twice stood unsuccessfully for Parliament as a Conservative candidate. After holding office for only a few months, Mr Gaffney was dismissed. It appears that he became involved in a major personality clash with influential councillors. The main allegation against him was rude behaviour.
   The Local Government Act 1972 made this incident possible. Previously, under Section 100 of the Local Government Act 1933, the Clerk of a county council could be dismissed only with ministerial consent. The 1972 Act withdrew this protection. Subordinate staff in local government have a right of appeal against dismissal in accordance with national agreements. Again, this safeguard does not extend to chief officers.
7. See p. 133 *supra.*
8. *Local Government Chronicle,* 14 December 1973. Unfortunately Greenwood's figures do not distinguish between English and Welsh non-metropolitan counties.
9. See p. 134 *infra.*
10. For a full account of the work of the Staff Commission, see pp. 128-34 *infra.*
11. See p. 71.
12. This breed of official documents began to appear in 1970. A Consultative Document, like a Green Paper, invites comment and advice. Unlike a Green Paper, it is normally not on sale at the Stationery Office because it is not aimed at the general public but at a specialised clientele. See Arthur Silkin, 'Green Papers and Changing Methods of Consultation', in *Public Administration* (Winter 1973), Vol. 51, pp. 427-48.
13. SI 373 of 1973: The Local Government Act 1972 (Commencement No. 1) (England) Order.
14. For a detailed account of experience at Bradford see Gerald Hodges in *Public Finance and Accountancy* (June 1974), pp. 182-8.
15. SI 1861 of 1973.

Chapter 4

RELATIONS BETWEEN COUNTIES
AND DISTRICTS

Methods of Co-operation
It is widely argued that the success of the new structure of local
government will depend on the quality of co-operation between
county and district. Both have a claim to represent local opinion,
albeit over different areas. They share functions, particularly planning, which cannot be exercised independently of each other. There
can be great advantages if they agree to share the use of more
specialised resources. Yet standing in the way of co-operation are
separate institutional loyalties, perhaps political differences and a
desire by small bodies to stay independent and avoid any feeling of
being swallowed up by Big Brother.

One effect of reorganisation was to reduce the number of elected
members serving on both district and county councils. As there are
now fewer councils, this was a natural outcome. The position varies.
Joint membership is common in the West Midlands but unusual in
Tyne and Wear. Some local Labour groups opposed double nominations. Elsewhere fewer people were willing to find the time needed
for dual membership. It is a moot point whether such direct links
are advantageous. Joint membership should ensure that the two tiers
are better informed of each other's position and so should promote
mutual understanding and co-ordination of policy formation. On
the other hand, where the same individuals serve on two councils
their loyalties may become divided and their opinions less certain.
The absence of common membership may cause a gap to develop
between the two tiers, but this can be partially bridged through
informal party activity by inviting local county councillors to attend
the caucus meetings of their district council colleagues.

Various means exist to facilitate county/district co-operation,
some of which depend on the 1972 Act and some of which do not.
Section 102 of the Act authorises two or more authorities to appoint
a joint committee for a particular purpose. Under Section 113 a
local authority may place its staff at the disposal of another authority, subject to consultation with the staff concerned. Alternatively,

one local council can enter into agreement with another to provide goods and services for it in accordance with the Local Authorities (Goods and Services) Act 1970. These provisions can facilitate joint purchasing, joint use of a computer or the employment of staff on a particular project. Section 101 of the 1972 Act gives a further opportunity for more sophisticated co-operation through agency arrangements. Under an agency agreement one local authority agrees to carry out functions on behalf of another subject to conditions covering control of general policy and control of expenditure. Agency differs from contractual arrangements in that it assumes that decisions will be made by the agent authority within the basic framework initially accepted. Thus where a county uses a district as its agent there is an element of decentralisation in decision-making and the role of the district is enhanced. In contrast, contractual agreements offer no delegation of discretion: work is carried out under instructions in return for payment. Agency involves a political decision: a contract can be merely a matter of administrative convenience.

A local authority, particularly a county, may decentralise its organisation by establishing local offices and depots. This makes its services more accessible to the public. Such action may not affect other councils; alternatively, it may be associated with the joint use of premises or the formation of local liaison or advisory committees designed to promote local participation in the decentralised service. The 1972 Act excluded the possibility of agency in relation to education and social services, so in regard to these functions the possibility of decentralisation becomes particularly important.

Closer relationships between the two tiers of local authorities can be promoted by the establishment of joint committees to discuss items of mutual interest. It is easy to accept this idea in a first rush of enthusiasm and optimism. But to find useful work for such committees to do can be much more difficult. They can have no executive powers. They can easily become a vehicle for minding other people's business. If a single committee is to cover a whole county then it can easily become a forum for complaints about county policy. If the county has the same number of representatives as each county district, then the county will be heavily outnumbered. If the county has equal representation with all the districts put together, then the burden of attendance on county councillors is heavy. If the county establishes a separate committee for each district, then the cost is heavy both in councillors' time and officers' time. If the membership is static it may not contain councillors with experience most appropriate for the agenda of a particular meeting. If the membership is fluid and can be adjusted to suit the business, then the committee tends to lose continuity and becomes a series of *ad hoc* gatherings. Problems of organisation of an all-county committee are also greater where there are a large number of districts in a county because the size of each meeting is bigger. Thus it is more difficult to organise county/district liaison meetings in Greater Manchester than in the other metropolitan counties.

A natural subject for county/district discussion would seem to be consideration of the long-term future of the area. There is a clear need to relate a county's strategic plan to local problems and aspirations. Yet such discussion must be carefully prepared to have positive results. The expense of regular meetings could be formidable if they are to bring together both councillors and the wide range of county and district officers who would need to be involved.

Agency

The concept of agency—that one authority may undertake work for another—certainly complicated the task of bringing the new structure of government into operation. Section 101 of the 1972 Act, which enables one local council to arrange for another to discharge its functions, does not mention the word agency. But it has been adopted by general consent as the appropriate legal term to cover this type of situation. In law the powers of an agent are restricted to those conferred on him by the principal. Therefore the element of discretion enjoyed by an agent depends on the details of the agreement under which the agency operates. Further, its duration also depends upon the agreement or, otherwise, on the will of the principal. It follows that the agent has no rights other than those in the covenant. This is a humble position, far more humble than that formerly enjoyed by local authorities exercising delegated powers under the Education Act 1944, the Town and Country Planning Act 1947 and the Local Government Act 1958.[1]

There was no reference to agency in the initial Conservative White Paper which outlined proposals for local government reform. There was no detailed discussion of the subject when the Local Government Bill was passing through the Commons. Agency was perhaps an embarrassing topic, convenient to avoid. As a complicating factor in a pattern of administration, agency simply does not fit the philosophy of a reform designed to modernise, streamline and make more efficient. Agency also carried with it the overtones of delegation which since 1944 had been an irritant in the relationships between county councils and the larger non-county boroughs and urban districts. On the other hand, to allow local councils to come to mutually satisfactory arrangements about helping each other and sharing responsibilities is to add to local freedom, to encourage local initiative and permit flexibility to suit local conditions.

A broad case in favour of agency can be made in terms of local democracy and participation. The Maud Committee on Management laid heavy stress on the idea that local authorities must be given a satisfying range of responsibilities if councillors and officials of high calibre are to be attracted to local government. The grant of agency powers should add to the attraction of service with a district council. It could also enable districts to co-ordinate services operated by agency with services conferred by statute directly upon them. However, this possibility is restricted because agency is not available for education or social services; thus the district responsibility for housing cannot be co-ordinated with the social services through this means. Agency does permit a fuller element of local participation in the administration of a county service. Knowledge of local problems becomes more readily available. Agency can also be of value in smoothing over transitional problems. In particular, new authorities like Avon, which lacked an established base and inherited few resources, needed initial assistance from its neighbours. And where the 1972 Act transferred a function from one class of authority to another it was often convenient for arrangements to be made to postpone the handover; this applied particularly to refuse disposal.

Any discussion of possible agency arrangements had to face two basic issues: the extent of the agency and the conditions governing its operation. The second of these is the more important in relation to how the scheme will work for it raises the question—how much discretion is to be left to the agent? At one extreme the principal may exercise detailed supervision over what is done on his behalf. At the other extreme the agent can be free to make decisions about the allocation of resources within an agreed budget. But how far will a principal (normally the county) be willing to surrender control of priorities, standards and appointments of staff? How far will a county accept that a district committee has a better appreciation of district needs?

An argument about the desirability of agency can be fitted into a form of cost-benefit analysis, but the analysis will give no precise results. It may be agreed that agency, or some lesser means of decentralisation, will increase cost, although the amount of the increase can be open to dispute. It may also be agreed that agency or decentralisation gives better service in the sense of greater sensitivity to local requirements; again the extent of this advantage may be controversial. While cost may be measured in terms of the currency unit there can be no precise measurement of the benefit of sensitivity. So whether any type of decentralisation is justified in relation to cost can only be decided on the basis of subjective assessments. The decisions made will reflect locality and political pressures.

The managerial case for agency rested on short-term considerations. It was sometimes convenient to continue existing procedures and use of office accommodation. At first, districts may have staff with the appropriate experience to carry out county functions, but this can be a wasting asset as recruitment of replacements becomes difficult and is probably uneconomic. NALGO is hostile to agency as it is felt to create uncertainty which adversely affects career prospects.[2] Thus an advertisement for a post, the duties of which depend wholly or partly on agency, may not get a good response. Of course, some security is offered by the practice of making agency agreements for a minimum period subject to renewal. Yet the length of the minimum period itself creates a problem: if it is too long, the future reshaping of administration can be delayed, while if it is short there is less reassurance for staff.

Elected representatives tend to consider agency in a political context, albeit not necessarily in a party sense. Indeed, the pressures depended largely on local loyalties and the time factor. Early discussions of the preparatory joint committees showed a tendency in some shires to think of agency as a useful means of promoting harmony with the districts and easing resentment at the advance of county control over the county boroughs. Some county chief officers were slow to formulate the case against agency either because they had given the matter insufficient thought or because they were contemplating retirement or because they were not confident of retaining their positions in the new organisation. The result was that some of the preliminary work envisaged a wider scale of agency than that which ultimately emerged. After the shadow authorities had been elected and their chief officers were appointed the county attitudes became firmer. At the final meeting of the Association of Municipal Corporations in September 1973 there were complaints that the county councils were trying to 'hog the action'. This atmosphere led to a large number of local disputes over agency.[3]

Because agency involves a transfer of responsibility between authorities it immediately raises issues of prestige. Had widespread agency been encouraged some districts certainly would have tried to regain the administration of services transferred to the shire counties by the 1972 Act. In particular, districts which contained or constituted former county boroughs would have sought to use agency as a means to retain some influence over education and the social services. Arguments would have been invoked about local democracy, the need for committees regulating personal services to have local knowledge and the convenience to the public of decentralised administration. But a wholesale handing back from counties to districts would have produced a patchwork of confusion and done much to vitiate the central purpose of the 1972 Act. So to prevent conflict arising over district attempts to 'claw back' education and social services, these two functions were specifically excluded from the permissible range of agency agreements.

The Government was aware that agency raised sensitive issues. After consultation with the associations of local authorities, Circular 131/72 was issued to provide general guidance on the subject. It noted that early decisions on agency were important especially where these had implications for staff. It also laid stress on the theme that agency should not be regarded as a means whereby a local authority could 'claw back' functions that had been lost in the reorganisation and so partially offset the effect of the Act. The Circular also emphasised that agency should not be organised so that counties were confined to the planning of services while leaving their execution in the hands of district councils.

'But equally there should be no presumption against agency arrangements simply because the statutory responsibility is allocated to a particular class of authority ... The objective should be to improve the effectiveness and democratic discharge of local government functions, thus benefiting both local government itself and the public whom it serves.'[4]

The Circular implied that this optimum could be achieved either by the district acting as agent for the county or *vice versa*. Sometimes detailed local knowledge that could be provided by district councillors was a major advantage. Alternatively, where an existing authority had developed a body of professional expertise, this specialised team-skill could be retained and utilised. Often the best use required operation over a large area. Further, the Circular stressed that agency functions should be considered in relation to the duties of a local authority as a whole. Related activities might be best conducted by a single council, e.g. in relation to the Town Development Act 1952. The Circular left open the question of whether staff operating agency should be employed by the principal or the agent authority.

Five functions were commended by the Circular as being particularly suitable for agency—highways, planning, refuse disposal, consumer protection and libraries. In the case of planning the Circular admitted that there was little scope for agency as the 1972 Act divided the planning function between counties and districts, a division which demanded close co-operation and would lead to formal and informal working arrangements between the two tiers. The amount of agency ultimately agreed for libraries[5] and consumer protection[6] proved to be limited. So its widest use was in relation to highways[7] and refuse disposal.[8]

The Circular recommended that agency agreements should cover the following points: extent of the agency and of the discretion allowed to the agent; arrangements relating to staff and property; duration and means of revising agreements; budgetary and financial control. Disputes arising over the issues were to be settled by the Secretary of State in accordance with Section 110 of the 1972 Act. This limited the Minister's power of decision to the period before 1 April 1974 and any directions he made are to expire after five years, i.e. on 31 March 1979. So after the initial period any agency agreements require the mutual consent of the participants.

The provision for ministerial arbitration was due to pressure at the Report stage of the Local Government Bill[9] when it was argued that the provisions for agency would be meaningless if the counties refused to co-operate. The new clause did not please any of the local authority associations. The County Councils Association claimed it would give districts an incentive to disagree with county proposals and so would stimulate conflict. How far this proved to be the case cannot be known since one cannot tell how districts might have reacted in different circumstances. The associations representing boroughs and districts regretted that ministerial powers extended only to a transitional period up to 1979. As it is, staff executing agency schemes may find that the pattern of their duties is changed at the will of an authority other than their employer. The safeguards for staff interests will protect them from adverse effects of change; nevertheless, the potentially temporary character of agency does cause uncertainty.

Circular 131/72 set out a timetable for the submission of agency disputes to the Department of the Environment. Formal notification was to be made by 17 September 1973 and the intention was that decisions should be made by 'early November'. Obviously this was an optimistic schedule and, in the event, it could not be maintained. Disputes were still being notified to the Department early in 1974 owing to the complexity of local negotiations. Finally the Department intimated it could not deal with any cases submitted after the end of February. The power of the Secretary of State to make directions about agency powers lapsed on 1 April. Some of his decisions were sent by the last post on 29 March—the last working day before the deadline.

Local negotiations had been lengthy because they involved delicate political, administrative and tactical considerations. Districts had to decide if they were going to ask for agency powers and, if so, how wide these should be. If the county failed to agree or offered a compromise solution, the districts had to decide whether to accept the county view, try and reach a better compromise or appeal to the Department. Since the latter's decision, even if favourable, had effect for only five years, the further question arose whether it was worthwhile to obtain powers for a short period since the county would almost certainly withdraw them after 1979. For counties the issues were even more complex. If the principle of agency was accepted, the questions were: how much agency? under what conditions? should all districts have equal treatment? if not, what are to be the criteria for differentiation? Unequal treatment of districts involved the creation of distinctions of status which smaller districts might resent especially if they could be taken to imply disparagement of the quality of staff. Where agreement was not reached the county had to consider whether the district would appeal and the probable consequences of such a move. Some districts made holding applications for a direction on agency as a bargaining counter while local negotiations continued. Occasionally this tactic succeeded and secured an adjustment of county policy. Certainly both districts and counties were under Government pressure to settle disputes locally. Mr Graham Page, Minister for Local Government and Development in the Conservative administration, was unusually emphatic on this matter when addressing the Society of Town Clerks at Brighton in June 1973. He commented on 'extraordinary acrobatics' when local government asked for both less government interference and more central help and guidance. 'Keep your feet out of Marsham Street',[10] Mr Page is reported to have advised the assembled town clerks; 'You come to us too many times. We give you matters to decide at local level and too many of you keep coming running to us.'

In spite of this advice a large number of disputes over agency were referred to government departments. The table below shows the number of firm as opposed to provisional or 'holding' applications for directions on agency. The publicity given to the reasons for the earlier DOE decisions may have encouraged local authorities to reach local agreements and so reduced the number of cases requiring ministerial judgement, particularly as some disputes were related to the conditions of agency rather than its extent. It will be seen that only a small proportion of applications were successful. Indeed, only the Department of the Environment gave any directions.

LOCAL GOVERNMENT ACT 1972
SECTION 110: AGENCY APPLICATIONS AND DECISIONS

Function	Department	Applications	Decisions	
			Direction	No direction
Highways	Environment	60	14	46
Traffic management or road safety	Environment	4	1	3
Planning	Environment	3	—	3
Refuse disposal	Environment	5	3	2
Weights and measures	Prices and Consumer Protection	5	—	5
Food and drugs	Agriculture	27	—	27
Libraries	Education	21	—	21
Explosives	Home Office	2	—	2
Totals		127	18	109

Decentralisation

The concept of decentralisation is far less precise than that of agency. It can take a variety of forms. At the minimum it requires dividing up an organisation so that sub-groups are responsible for the work in separate locations. This can be merely a matter of convenience without any policy implications. Alternatively, local offices may be provided to facilitate public access to a service. Decentralisation of this kind is not confined to counties, for metro-politan districts have local offices dealing with local welfare services and housing. Where a county has local offices these may involve co-operation with districts, e.g. through sharing accommodation in the same building. Again this can lead to formal and informal consul-tation between county and district staff. The next step up the scale of co-operation is for a county to have some form of joint consulta-tive committee with one or more district councils to give advice on county services. The ultimate form of decentralisation is a type of partnership where district councillors share in making decisions on a county function. Particularly in the case of highways, some counties offered their districts a decentralisation scheme as an alternative to agency.

Staffordshire is one example of a county with an extensive system of local advisory committees. Each of its nine districts has separate committees for libraries, highways, social services and planning. In addition, five area advisory committees have been established for the career guidance services. These committees comprise representatives from the county and district councils, and are intended to strengthen links between the County, the districts and the public. Certainly they are expensive in terms of the time of both councillors and officers. This type of arrangement need not necessarily operate in the context of the two tiers of local authorities. Stockport Metropolitan District has established area committees which report to its own functional committees.

In Devon the concept of area decentralisation has been carried even further. This is a reflection both of its large physical size and the substantial growth caused by its extension into three county boroughs, which nearly doubled the population of the administrative county. No doubt the scheme of area administration was supported by a variety of motives. The County wished to minimise resentment felt by county boroughs at the loss of their independence; the county borough representatives felt it would be an advantage if as many matters as possible could be settled locally without reference to County Hall; county borough staff saw area administration as an opportunity to improve their job prospects in the new system. So a plan was adopted to divide Devon into four sectors with area offices based on Exeter, Plymouth, Torbay and Barnstaple. A series of area committees has been established, with a membership of district and county councillors. Those for education and the social services are essentially advisory. The planning and transportation committees have some delegated executive powers. A number of county area officers, including area secretaries, have been appointed with the status of deputy chief officers. But the whole system has to work within the framework of county policy and the county budget.

This style of administration is open to a number of difficulties and objections. It is expensive, particularly in relation to the salary levels of senior officers. In Devon it has been impossible to design the areas satisfactorily. The need for simplicity demands that county area boundaries shall not transgress district boundaries. Devon has accepted this principle, but one result is that the area immediately west of Exeter in the Teignbridge District comes within the County's Torbay administrative area. There have also been problems in finding accommodation for area offices; the Plymouth area offices are in Plympton. So area administration is not always as convenient for the public as one might have hoped. The area secretaries are also in a slightly curious position. There is some suggestion that they have a general responsibility for the effectiveness of county services in their area, but the area offices of each department, e.g. education, certainly feel answerable to the headquarters of their own department at County Hall and not to the area secretary. And since the area secretaries report to the County Secretary and not the Chief Executive it is quite clear that they are not mini-chief executives; instead they are left with legal and secretarial duties combined with some responsibility for public relations and for acting as a channel of communication between the County and its districts.

Other forms of county/district integration were envisaged in schemes prepared for planning in Somerset and highways in Surrey. The Somerset plan was that the County and its districts should work together to provide a unified planning service with a unified staff. The arrangement was intended to overcome the division of responsibility for planning caused by the 1972 Act. The Somerset Joint Committee accepted a scheme under which a third of the County Planning Committee was to be nominated by the districts: similarly a third of the membership of each district planning committee would be nominated by the County Council. District committees would have delegated to them all county planning functions except matters relating to a National Park (i.e. Exmoor), matters concerning more than one district and matters substantially affecting the interests of the County. All planning staff were to be employed by the County with the cost shared equally between the County and the districts. Yeovil did not accept this scheme but the other authorities prepared to operate it. Had it worked well, the experiment might have been copied elsewhere. However, it largely broke down in November 1973 for a variety of reasons. Some of the chief officers and elected representatives who had provided the impetus for co-operation were ceasing to hold office. New men, particularly newly appointed chief executives, were less keen on the plan. Political control on the County Council had changed from Independent to Conservative; this was said to have led to less flexibility and greater emphasis on precise business-like methods. It was also argued that as the 1972 Act had given development control to the districts, the Joint Committee scheme was designed to circumvent the will of Parliament. Ultimately when the County prepared a formal document to implement the policy statement of the Joint Committee, the balance of district opinion found it unacceptable as being biased in the County's favour. So the partnership scheme largely collapsed and, except for West Somerset and Taunton Deane, the districts took up their statutory functions on 1 April 1974.

The Surrey partnership scheme for highways did come into effect. As an alternative to agency, Surrey offered its districts a form of partnership which involved a share in making decisions about both county and district functions. After extensive negotiations seven districts opted for a limited agency arrangement while four chose partnership. These four, Guildford, Mole Valley, Tandridge and Waverley, form the southern and less densely populated part of the County. Each has a highway sub-committee of the County Council; the district nominates eight members, the County nominates nine and the chairman must be a county member. These sub-committees have wide delegated powers. However, they must observe the programmes, policies, codes of practice and specifications of the County Highways Committee and they must not incur expenditure beyond that sanctioned by estimates. Land for highway purposes cannot be purchased unless it is included in the County's programme. There is also a reserve power for the County Highways Committee to issue directions to an area sub-committee. The actual highway work is carried out by county staff but the servicing of the committees, at least initially, is being done by district staff at district expense.

This partnership scheme is not unlike arrangements which had existed in Surrey before reorganisation in relation to planning, education and health and welfare services.[11] In contrast with agency, this form of partnership offers less scope for professional and manual staff of the district but arguably more scope for councillors. Under agency, district councillors are limited by the extent of the agency which normally excludes major capital works: under partnership nothing within the county programme for the district is beyond the ambit of the area sub-committee.

Decentralisation affects staff in that it requires some to be stationed at local offices and so may cause travelling or possibly residential problems. But the effect on career prospects is less than under agency where the individual officer may be uneasy because the basis of his employment is impermanent and because another authority is making major decisions which affect his work. Decentralisation is particularly extensive in relation to social services due to the strong need for easy public accessibility to the source of aid. Some shires have established a three-tier system for dealing with this function. The headquarters department is concerned with general policy, finance and future planning; area offices are responsible for the supervision of the services provided; local offices enable the public to meet the staff and provide a base from which the daily work is organised. There is likely to be pressure for the establishment of further local offices, and not only for the social welfare services. The hindrance to this development is largely a question of cost and shortage of suitable accommodation, although in some areas decentralisation has been encouraged by shortage of accommodation at headquarters.

Clearly, the nature of decentralisation depends on whether it is associated with some form of local committee with advisory or executive powers. Counties vary in the extent to which they welcome this extra element of local representation. Where such committees exist there is added opportunity for local participation in administration with a chance to press local needs. Without the committees, decentralisation becomes entirely an executive matter, a question of convenience which may help to speed up some types of decision. Counties also vary in the extent to which they have uniform areas for the management of their decentralised services. In Devon, as shown above, the County is organised through four subdivisions which cover most county services. Hampshire, in contrast. has different units for each function: social services are organised through three, education through eight and libraries through thirteen area organisations. The Devon model with its cohesive units raises the possibility that decentralisation might extend to planning future development of services, perhaps with different areas in favour of different priorities. This could be defended in terms of a healthy democratic reaction against uniformity and remote county control. Alternatively it could be seen as a move towards breaking up larger authorities and thus contrary to the *raison d'être* of the 1972 Act.

Contract Arrangements

A local authority can arrange with another for the supply of goods or services under the Local Authorities (Goods and Services) Act 1970. Similarly one authority may place its staff at the disposal of another, subject to consultation with the officers concerned; this is provided for by Section 113 of the Local Government Act 1972. Such contracts are made in the interests of economical and efficient administration. They are essentially a managerial convenience. There is no question here of sharing policy decisions : as in a normal business transaction, the customer specifies the nature of his requirements. The authority that provides the supply is interested in the amount of payment received in relation to cost and in the effect of the transaction on its organisation. A contract agreement is unlikely to stir much controversy unless some councillors feel that their authority should be wholly separate from and independent of its neighbours.

Contracts can facilitate the purchase of goods at cheaper rates through bulk orders. They can ensure that expensive equipment, e.g. a computer, is used to the fullest advantage. They can ensure that specialised staff are fully occupied, and can be of particular use in the case of staff who have variable workloads, e.g. architects and valuers. In a period of reorganisation they can be of great value where one authority is short of accommodation or specialised staff while adjacent authorities, which perhaps have lost territory or functions, have resources surplus to present requirements. This situation applies where one county has been formed out of others, e.g. Avon and Somerset and Gloucester, or where a county has united with a large county borough.

There can be particular advantages in sharing the employment of architects. They provide a service not necessarily related to a particular function or committee and this accentuates their professional independence. Their workload tends to be variable as it expands and contracts with the scale of the local building programme. At periods of heavy pressure extra help may be obtained either from other local authorities or by engaging architects in private practice. DOE Circular 56/73 urged co-operation between counties and districts, especially in relation to special skills. Interchange of staff, it argued, would give valuable additional experience, notably to architects from the smaller districts who otherwise would be largely restricted to housing projects. Joint county-district architectural teams could provide more harmonious treatment for new district housing estates in relation to buildings constructed for county purposes, i.e. schools, libraries and old people's homes. Such joint teams could perhaps more readily plan for the joint use of buildings, in particular the use of schools out of school hours.

In practice, co-operation has been sometimes easier to arrange between counties and their largest districts, notably the former county boroughs, rather than with the smaller districts. The latter have more limited functions and resources; they may be even keener to assert independence. From the county viewpoint, the concentration by the districts on housing can lead to a feeling that architects from second-tier authorities have little to contribute to design problems arising from county responsibilities. The situation of former county boroughs is different. They were faced with a wide loss of duties, in particular education, social services and personal health, which cut down drastically their architectural work. The situation could be met with a number of remedies. One was for some of the county borough staff to move to the county. Another was for the county borough staff to move to the county *en bloc* and for the district architectural work to be done by the county on a contract basis. The third possibility was for staff to remain undisturbed and for the design of county buildings within the district, and possibly outside it, to be undertaken by the district on a contract basis.

Of these broad choices, the first may appear the simplest. However, it could create substantial problems. Established teams of professional staff are broken up. Specialists who are caring for a project are moved away long before it has been completed. There are accommodation problems, not merely for staff moving house but also for the receiving authority—architects and their drawing boards demand a great deal of space which might well not be available at the county headquarters. If arrangements are made for them to remain in district offices, then the county architect's department becomes dispersed. The second solution, that the district should surrender altogether its architectural service, avoids some of these problems but not all. It is also open to a policy objection: a district may not be willing to reduce further the scale of its activities. The third solution, that the district contracts to do work for the county, offers a minimum of immediate disturbance. But it does require the Chief Architect of a district to be responsible to two masters. He must ensure that the time and priority of attention of his staff is shared fairly beween county and district. The district council must accept that in relation to much of the work of its architectural staff, the district interest is only to see that the district is adequately paid for the service provided. There are two major objections to this kind of arrangement. It demands good working relationships between the professional staffs of the local authorities involved; should tensions develop, the scheme could scarcely work well. It is also impermanent, based on an agreement for a limited term of years subject to renewal. So while the staff are spared upheaval in 1974 there must be doubt about the future. It is arguable that a contractual agreement of this type merely postpones reorganisation. However, Hampshire, Portsmouth and Southampton made a scheme on these lines.

Concurrent Powers

The Local Government Act 1972 contained provisions for a considerable range of powers to be concurrent between counties and districts in both metropolitan and non-metropolitan areas. They cover museums, art galleries, acquisition and disposal of land for planning purposes, development or redevelopment, clearance of derelict land, country parks, caravan sites, health education, provision for recreation including parks and swimming baths, entertainments, aerodromes and action in case of natural emergencies. The list does not contain the major local services but it does, in total, amount to a substantial opportunity to improve the quality of life.

There are very considerable contrasts in how these powers are being used. Art galleries provide a simple example. Greater Manchester has decided that art galleries shall be a district function. Neighbouring Merseyside has taken the opposite view so that the famous Walker Gallery in Liverpool has become a county responsibility.

Concurrent powers offer a chance of healthy co-operation between the two tiers of local authorities. Alternatively they can cause duplication, argument or inaction. The danger of inaction arises from the possibility that a council may lose enthusiasm for a service in the hope that the responsibility may be accepted by the other tier. There is evidence that some districts, both metropolitan and non-metropolitan, have lessened their interest in museums because if the county takes over the local museum the cost can be more widely shared. In contrast, derelict land can stimulate competitive action: Birmingham and the West Midlands were quickly at loggerheads over their proposals for derelict sites. South Yorkshire wished to take over the Doncaster country park and was repulsed.

One way of avoiding disputes over concurrent powers is for the two tiers to strike a bargain. It may be agreed that the county does X while districts do Y. Thus in Tyne and Wear the arrangement is that the county shall be responsible for museums and art galleries while the districts have sole control of the provision of leisure facilities involving physical exertion, unless a district asks the county to take over a major project which will be of importance beyond the district.

In several areas one of the most delicate topics in county/district negotiations was the future of the local airport. Before the 1972 Act these had often been a borough rather than a county responsibility. There was an element of prestige and possibly of commercial advantage associated with a municipal airport. Yet almost all were unremunerative and were, or threatened to be, a burden on the local rate. The 1972 Act gave the counties a wider concern with transportation and it was natural that they should wish to share in or take over completely the municipal undertakings. County involvement also ensured that any financial loss would be borne over a wider area. However, county opinion is not always united especially if there are area tensions. Plymouth has ambitions to develop a local airport; now it has to help to subsidise that at Exeter, which it sees as a rival, through the medium of the county rate. The recasting of airport ownership and administration caused complex negotiations and there is variety in the outcome. There are doubts about whether some will continue due both to financial liabilities and also to unpopularity with local residents through noise. A district will not wish to hand over valuable airport property to a county if there is any chance that the latter will close it down and use the site for a fresh purpose. So although Merseyside has taken over Liverpool's Speke airport it has agreed that any part ceasing to be used for airport purposes should be returned to Liverpool. These negotiations dragged on until the very last moment: the future of Speke after Sunday 31 March 1974 was not finally decided until a special meeting of the Merseyside County Council held on the preceding Friday afternoon.

NOTES

1. For a full discussion of the distinction between delegation and agency see Peter G. Richards, *Delegation in Local Government* (Allen & Unwin, 1956), Ch. III.
2. Glyn Phillips, Chairman of NALGO's Local Government Committee, made this comment on agency: 'It means that a person's working responsibility is split in two directions: the local authority that employs him and the remote external body which really determines his pay, conditions and area of duties. He has no scope for advancement in his employing authority, yet is left out of the main career ladder of the (other) body; he will be in the middle of any friction between the two, but his own interests will always come last in the queue since neither will regard them as their responsibility.' *The Guardian*, 13 June 1973.
3. See pp. 83–4.
4. Circular 131/72, para. 11.
5. See pp. 109–10 *infra*.
6. See p. 96 *infra*.
7. See pp. 102–6 *infra*.
8. See p. 122 *infra*.
9. HC Deb., Vol. 841, cols 244–65. See also HL Deb., Vol. 335, cols 759–81 when the new clause was introduced.

10. The local government division of the Department of the Environment is situated in Marsham Street.
11. On health and welfare administration in Surrey, see R. S. B. Knowles in *Public Administration* (Spring 1950), Vol. XXVIII, pp. 31–6.

Chapter 5

FUNCTIONS

This chapter consists of a series of short commentaries on how the Local Government Act influenced most of the main spheres of local authority activity. Quite deliberately no attempt has been made to create a common design for these essays. Each service is treated in the way best suited to its own situation.

Not all functions are included. Housing is the chief omission. The research on which this work is based concentrated on the counties and the metropolitan districts. To discuss housing problems solely in the context of metropolitan areas could give a misleading picture. In the metropolitan areas concern for the homeless is divided between the Housing and Social Services Departments of the districts; in shire counties there is the further division of responsibility between county social services and district housing. Whether this split between the two tiers aggravates the problem of homelessness is a subject that should receive detailed study.

One other general introductory point must be made. Reorganisation creates pressure for more even standards of service. Where two or more authorities have been merged together the new authority may find that different policies have been followed in different sectors of its area. Any move towards equality will mean that those places which had enjoyed more generous provision of particular services must now wait for further progress on these services until the remainder of the new authority has caught up. Leading examples can be found in highway maintenance, school maintenance and facilities for residential care. Another way of sharing more equally is to ensure that specialised services are made available to a larger area. Reorganisation has made this possible. But if there is no increase in available resources, more benefit for some places involves a poorer service for others. These general considerations apply to all the functions discussed in this chapter: to avoid repetition they are not stressed in each of the following sections.

Consumer Protection

The phrase consumer protection has but recently achieved wide use in local government.[1] Yet if the name is new the origins of the function can be traced back to legislation fixing standards for weights and measures. By the nineteenth century two aspects of consumer protection had been firmly established as responsibilities of local government. They were the safeguarding of health through stopping the sale of noxious substances and the prevention of fraud.

In the days before pre-packaging, checks on the accuracy of weights and measures were a major deterrent against fraud. Now with packed and branded goods often promoted by massive advertising, the need is to ensure that goods are fairly described and that the customer does not suffer from over-zealous selling techniques. The phrase 'consumer protection' has emerged partly through greater public consciousness of these matters but also because the requirements needed to meet the current situation have changed almost dramatically. A Cabinet Minister has been given responsibility for consumer affairs since 1972. New legislation in this field appears each year.

While Section 201 of the Local Government Act 1972 gave responsibility for consumer protection to the counties, the districts have concurrent powers in relation to food hygiene. Previously the distribution of functions was very confused. Weights and measures had belonged to the counties and county boroughs, but non-county boroughs and urban districts in excess of 60,000 population could claim to exercise these duties. Further, any county district irrespective of size could be given these powers by a ministerial order. The food and drugs authorities were the counties and county boroughs together with the non-county boroughs and urban districts above 40,000 population. Similarly the Consumer Protection Acts 1961 and 1971 were administered by counties, county boroughs and the larger county districts. There was also variety of practice as to which department of an authority undertook these duties. In urban authorities it was common for food and drugs legislation to be enforced by the Health Department whereas in counties the task went to the Weights and Measures Department. Legislation regarding safety precautions for petroleum and explosives was generally enforced by Weights and Measures but sometimes by the fire brigade. In regard to analysts, some authorities employed their own; some used the services of another local council; some employed private consultants. Another cause of variation was that some statutory powers were not—or not yet—utilised by some councils. This applied particularly to the provision of a consumer advisory service, the Trading Stamps Act 1964, the Advertisements (Hire Purchase) Act 1967 and the Unsolicited Goods and Services Act 1971. And before reorganisation there had been little time to take much action over the Fair Trading Act 1973 and the Supply of Goods (Implied Terms) Act 1973.

So the task of the Consumer Protection Departments in the reorganised authorities was threefold. Work done in separate places had to be brought together in a larger organisation. Work done previously in separate departments of the same authority had to be co-ordinated. The obligations and opportunities of recent legislation had to be faced.

In these circumstances there was a clear case for simplifying the allocation of powers. But the loss of functions by boroughs and urban districts caused vigorous claims that the loss be offset by agency agreements. DOE Circular 131/72 had made some rather half-hearted suggestions as to the consumer protection functions that might be suitable for agency; these amounted to little more than allowing districts to prosecute traders for alleged breaches of the law and encouraging district cooperation in establishing consumer advice centres. Under pressure some counties did make limited agency agreements. Elsewhere there were disputes between counties and districts that were referred to Ministers. Five applications for directions to grant agency in relation to weights and measures went to the Department of Prices and Consumer Protection. Twenty-seven applications relating to food and drugs went to the Ministry of Agriculture. All were refused.

The case against agency in this area is a strong one. The number of qualified enforcement officers is limited; if they were divided up among the districts, at least in the shire counties, the teams would be very small and unable to specialise. A unified county service gives a better career structure and permits more flexible use of resources. Thus a larger organisation can better meet the needs of seaside areas which have a greatly increased population at holiday periods. The role of elected representatives in this service is not as important as might be expected. Complaints from the public are vital to the enforcement of trading standards but they tend to come direct from individuals and not via councillors. Other arguments against agency are the need for county-wide consistency on policy over sampling and prosecutions. It seems undesirable that a committee of district councillors should have to decide whether or not to institute legal proceedings against a local trader.

A question allied to agency is the extent to which the consumer protection service should be decentralised. To have more local divisional offices is more expensive but it is more convenient for the public. However, in many areas a high percentage of complaints are received not from personal calls at offices but by post and phone. This could suggest that the existence of local offices is not of the highest importance. Yet since writing and using the telephone tend to be middle-class skills, the lack of a visible reception point for complaints may tend to restrict the notification of grievances to those who find it easiest to express themselves. Contact with the public may be better facilitated through advice bureaux in shopping centres rather than through divisional offices which are sub-units of the central county organisation. While it is useful to multiply the avenues for complaint, the complaints themselves may be investigated most effectively through a strong unified team of enforcement officers.

Consumer protection still has a low status in county authorities, especially the shires. This is reflected in committee structures where the service usually comes within the ambit of the Public Protection Committee which has a variety of other responsibilities. Similarly, the chief officer is not a member of the management team save in those authorities where all chief officers nominally belong to the management team. There are other departments that are barred from this inner cabinet—the police, the fire service and the library. But these are long established and the need to maintain them at a high standard is generally appreciated. The old Weights and Measures Departments are still evolving into a much wider role covering trading standards and advice to consumers; the nature of this change and the need for it are less well understood. No doubt, if the system of corporate management works according to theory, the interests of consumer protection will be fully safeguarded wherever its affairs are discussed within a local authority. Nevertheless, exclusion from the top table is a sensitive matter and has implications of status.

Education
It is tempting to argue that reorganisation made little difference to the education service. Schools and colleges continued in the summer term of 1974 as if nothing had happened. In the following academic year the effects on scholastic work were less than dramatic. Some changes that were made, e.g. in education budgets, tended to reflect national economic pressures as much as changes in administrative boundaries.

Reform in education takes much time to come to fruition. Argument over what should be done is followed by planning details of the

D

agreed scheme. Then follows a quest for resources to carry out necessary works followed by the actual construction. As the new facilities become available existing courses have to be phased out slowly in order to avoid undue discontinuity in the education of particular age-groups. So if the reshaping of local government does cause major changes of organisation it will be some time before the full effects are apparent.

The complexity of the situation facing each new education authority depended upon the number of former education authorities included within its area. The table below shows the relationship betweeen the old and the new. It will be seen that the shire counties had a much wider variety of experience; over one-quarter suffered no change while Cumbria and Lancashire had to harmonise no fewer than six systems.

COMPOSITION OF EDUCATION AUTHORITIES

Number of former LEAs included in whole or part in new LEA	Shire counties	Metropolitan districts
1	10	3
2	7	28
3	11	5
4	8	—
5	1	—
6	2	—
Totals	39	36

The three metropolitan districts based on a single former authority were very different in character. Liverpool and Wolverhampton continued unchanged with the resources of the former county boroughs. The third district, Knowsley, consists of three urban districts and parts of two rural districts which were all in Lancashire. While Knowsley inherited from Lancashire all the buildings, staff and other educational resources based within its area, the administrative core of the new education authority had to be developed afresh.

Reorganisation brought together local authorities which had followed separate and conflicting patterns of school organisation. The difference could be over the age of transfer from one type of institution to another; over the method of selection for secondary education; over the provision of single-sex or mixed schools; over the support of direct grant schools. There was no particular urgency in dealing with some of these disparities. It matters little if children move from infant to junior schools at the age of seven in one part of an authority's domain while it is eight in another part. But the issue of secondary selection is more sensitive and confused. Former authorities had not necessarily applied the same policy everywhere in their territory. This was true even among the smallest ones: Westmorland had had comprehensive schools in rural areas but maintained the selective grammar school tradition in Kendal. Where councils with conflicting policies over the eleven-plus examination were combined, there was pressure to create a uniform system. Variations in local practice did not always follow the predictable political pattern: at Leicester the Labour controlled County Borough with selective grammar schools was united with an anti-Labour County which for years had operated a comprehensive system. Reorganisation will help to stimulate change in such places. Yet the nature of change will also depend upon the nature of the central government. The decisions made after April 1974 about the organisation of secondary schools will depend more on the political complexion of the government and the availability of resources than on geographical changes in local administration.

The immediate effect on schools and colleges was not on teaching but on the supporting services including the maintenance of buildings and grounds, supplies, appointments, payroll and the work of subject advisers. Where former education authorities had been amalgamated the new authority was bequeathed a variety of policies and practices. Capitation grants to schools for the purchase of supplies were often fixed at different levels. Sometimes, as at Brighton, the gap had been widened because a council had greatly increased these allowances immediately prior to reorganisation. The disparities could be ironed out by raising the lower scales to the higher scales. Alternatively, lower scales could be raised part of the way while the higher ones were frozen, in the expectation that further increases for the former would soon be justified by inflation. Unequal rules about fees payable by individuals, e.g. for music coaching, required more immediate action. Similarly the rules covering the payment of various supplementary grants had to be made uniform.

There could also be differences affecting the conditions of service for teachers, possibly over the criterion for having a free school lunch or whether a teacher attending a training course should be replaced. Another important inequality related to staff/pupil ratios where a former authority had made more generous provision either overall or at particular institutions. The normal solution to such problems was to try and improve standards by levelling upwards. Staff/pupil ratios cannot be readily adjusted in this way because of the cost. Any programme of reallocating staff within an authority to obtain a more equal distribution of resources had to be approached with caution. Teachers have differing skills and are not readily transferable from post to post. To proclaim that staffing standards in particular schools should be cut would be to invite a storm of protest from teachers, parents, local councillors and the governors or managers, especially where the schools belonged previously to a smaller education authority whose extinction was resented. If, as is quite likely, the favoured school was a selective grammar school, the protest would rapidly acquire political overtones.

The subject advisers could be redeployed more rapidly. Schools of the smaller former authorities soon had a much wider range of these services. The catchment areas of the specialised educational establishments were extended and much of the administrative work associated with out-county payments disappeared. There was more unification in the ordering of supplies in order to obtain the benefits of bulk purchase; as a consequence there was less opportunity for teachers to express preferences for materials and equipment. Holidays tended to become identical throughout an authority's area: again this could mean less flexibility for individual schools. Where divisional education offices were established, particularly in the former county boroughs, teachers had to adjust to working with the decentralised system and to learn what the local office could and could not decide. Specialised enquiries, for example on income tax, might be dealt with at an address other than that of the local office or the headquarters.

The loss of education powers caused more distress to the defunct county boroughs than the loss of any other function. Divisional executives which had operated restricted delegated powers under the aegis of the counties were also grieved at going out of existence. Partly to soothe such feelings some shire counties have established divisional advisory committees to work in conjunction with their divisional education offices. Such committees may form part of a larger scheme of area committees as in Devon and Staffordshire or they may stand alone as in Hampshire. The eight divisional committees in Hampshire are notable for the broad base of their constitution: only 10 per cent of the membership is nominated by the County Council and the remainder represent the district councils, governors and managers, churches, teachers, parents, employers' organisations, adult education, community and youth services as well as post fifth-form students. The intention appears to be to create a forum for the ventilation of ideas and local problems and, presumably, for the explanation of county policy.

County boroughs had greater reason to complain over their loss of powers since the reorganisation created fresh anomalies. Education authorities had been shut down to fit the fresh pattern of two-tier administration: it was not always a matter of size because some new education authorities are much smaller than some which disappeared. The three metropolitan districts not based on a former county borough, Knowsley, Tameside and Trafford, each have a population a little above or below 200,000, so they are much smaller than many places which lost education functions. Indeed, it is arguable that none of these three constitutes a separate, identifiable urban community of a kind that is comparable with any of the former county boroughs.

At Knowsley, Tameside and Trafford the task was to build a wholly new education authority. Schools, colleges and teachers were inherited from Cheshire and Lancashire. Some administrative and clerical staff were recruited from the divisional offices of the two counties, but these offices had exercised limited functions so the staff were not experienced in some of the duties of a full education authority, e.g. the assessment of grants. Subject advisers had to be recruited and there were inevitable problems over office accommodation.[2]

Metropolitan districts have a general need to develop co-operation in relation to specialised facilities, e.g. field centres and youth orchestras. There is a danger that metropolitan districts will avoid organising activities on a county-wide scale lest this should be used as an argument for the transfer of educational functions to the metropolitan counties. Partly because of the county threat, district councillors and officials are keen to establish a reputation for being progressive educational administrators.

Counties which lost educational resources to the metropolitan districts found the slimming process painful. Perhaps it caused resentment. This could explain the behaviour of one shire county which refused to pass over to metropolitan districts the personal files relating to teachers employed in the areas transferred.

All education authorities were affected by the concept of corporate planning through a management team of chief officers. This move was seen by many as a check on the independence of Education Departments. In one shire county the management team made a rule that only chief officers could attend: no deputies were admitted. It was feared that otherwise the County Education Officer would regularly send his deputy and so evade personal commitment to any recommendations made by the management team that were adverse to the interests of his department. The scale and cost of education had tended to create a unique status for it within a local authority. Under the philosophy of corporate planning this separatism will be restricted, with other chief officers having some concern for the development of the education service in harmony with other activities of their local authority.[3]

Highways
Section 187 of the 1972 Act split highway powers between counties and districts. This division, combined with widespread local agency arrangements, means that the pattern of responsibility for highway maintenance is now more varied and complex than that for any other local service.

Counties are the major highway authorities. Districts can claim to maintain unclassified roads in urban areas, i.e. the former boroughs and urban districts; this right is subject to cost limits fixed by the county council. District status in relation to highways derives from the wide highway powers previously exercised by urban authorities: county boroughs had had full responsibility, while urban councils cared for unclassified roads and those with a population above 20,000 could claim to maintain county highways. Counties are now responsible for local traffic orders including the control of parking but districts have concurrent powers, with county consent, to provide off-street car parks.

The problems of highway maintenance were submerged in many areas by controversy about agency. The specialised arguments are considered below but too often the conflict was aggravated by considerations of prestige. The small print of agency agreements must vary but they run broadly on the following lines.[4] They are limited in duration, usually of five years. The county establishes some form of cost control, probably by fixing in advance an agreed amount for maintenance expenditure per mile of road, the amount depending upon the character of the highway. Special items of road maintenance are to be agreed separately from the basic programme, the district to submit a list of these special items in order of priority for county approval. Other expenditure, e.g. on administration, has to be based on estimates approved by the county. Virement within estimates is also subject to county consent. Staff engaged on agency functions are employed by the district. All work has to be carried out to county standards and the County Surveyor has the right to undertake inspections to ensure that these standards have been attained. The County Treasurer has access to records for the purposes of audit. The agent, i.e. the district, may be required to join in county contracts for the supply of goods and services.

The case for agency powers over highways is greatly strengthened by the fact that all districts, save those consisting wholly of former rural districts, are entitled to highway functions of their own. They need equipment, manual workers and professional engineering staff to carry out and supervise these operations. They also need engineering and supporting staff to enable them to perform other statutory duties in relation to housing, sewerage, refuse collection, street cleansing, building inspection and local improvement schemes. Such staff can operate more economically and have a better career structure if given additional scope in highways. These considerations encouraged districts to try and obtain agency powers over the maintenance of county roads. A case could be made to show that some transfer of county responsibilities was needed to buttress district technical service departments which otherwise might be too small to be efficient. In addition, the districts argued that there was considerable public interest in local highway matters shown by reporting complaints and hazards. Agency would facilitate closer contact with the public and more immediate and perhaps more sympathetic response to their requests. Agency, it was claimed, would provide a better service at no greater cost.

However the case against agency is formidable. Counties are the highway authorities for all roads; districts have only a limited role. There should be but one standard within a county for the design and maintenance of roads: under agency arrangements there has to be some supervision by county staff to ensure that these standards are respected and this scrutiny tends to involve duplicate attention by professional staff of the county and the district. The Marshall Report on highway maintenance suggested that larger authorities were noticeably more efficient in this field,[5] and that the division and dispersal of expertise produces no economies of scale. Indeed, such diversion could produce a lowering of standards, particularly as highway engineering requires increasingly sophisticated support services. In terms of career opportunities the counties can attract better staff. And to counter the district claim about close relations with the public, it was argued that agency arrangements would exclude county councillors from taking an active part in highway administration in certain patches of the county.

So long as highways and transportation are considered in isolation, the balance of advantage is clearly against agency. Yet we are now in a period when it is fashionable to assert that local government functions must not be treated in isolation from each other. When highways are related to the other services a district can and must provide, it becomes clear that highway agency can be a powerful reinforcement of the second-tier authority and so help it with a wide range of other responsibilities. So the concept of agency has been quite widely adopted, especially in the case of districts which contain large ex-urban authorities and therefore have much experience of highway work. Of the fifty disputes submitted to the DOE over highway agency, fourteen were settled in favour of the districts.

Thus not all the second-tier authorities were treated alike. Hampshire is a useful example. Seven of its thirteen districts have full agency for highway maintenance, four have agency for part of their area while two have none at all. The seven authorities in the first category are wholly or largely urban in character and had substantial resources for highway work in both staff and equipment. The two districts in the third category were rural apart from small urban communities; their highway resources were frail. The difficulties were greatest in the intermediate category where the districts are largely rural but have at least one substantial urban area. Here some districts claimed either that agency should cover the whole of the territory or at least a larger part of it than the County would accept. One example is the New Forest District where Hampshire offered agency for the Lymington area while the District wanted agency for the whole of its domain: this would have placed some of the county staff under district control so Hampshire would not agree. In the Test Valley District agency was offered for Andover but the District asked for the Romsey area to be included since Romsey as a former non-county borough, although very small, did have some highways resources. The Hampshire view was that the roads in Romsey were insufficient to provide an economic unit for maintenance work. In both these cases the county view ultimately prevailed.

Road improvements are a separate matter. It is open to the counties to argue that district boundaries may be irrelevant to a major improvement scheme. Further, a large construction project would impose an unbearable but temporary load of work on the professional and administrative staff of the agent. The usual arrangement is to impose a cost limit so that within this ceiling the agent will deal with an improvement scheme while above the limit the county retains responsibility. The larger the size of the agent, the higher the ceiling is likely to be and the obvious cause for dispute is at what figure the limit should be set. The district agents may also feel aggrieved if the county refuses to pass over a project where the estimated cost falls just beyond the dividing line.

Other ancillary functions that may be included in highway agency are private street works, new streets and traffic management including speed limits, school crossing patrols, traffic signs, street playgrounds and car parking. Districts may also deal with litigation, including prosecutions for highway offences and the recovery of costs of damage to highway property. Road safety may also come within an agency agreement.[6] In holiday centres there is considerable interest in the environmental aspect of highways: it is important that the roadside should be attractive. Two Cornish districts, Kerrier and Restormel, have limited agency for highway maintenance over part of their areas but complete agency for grass cutting, tree planting, landscaping and roadside flower beds. At Restormel it is further agreed that the District may carry out work to a higher standard than that agreed with the County provided that the District meets the excess cost.

Some shires have no highway agency at all. There are three possible reasons for this situation. Either the county strongly opposed agency or the districts did not press for it or their requests to the DOE that the latter should instruct the county to grant agency were unsuccessful. Some districts did not exercise their right under Section 187 to care for some or all of their unclassified urban roads. In a small market town in a predominantly rural area the urban roads are a small oasis amid a large mileage of county highways. To maintain a separate district highways organisation here could well be an uneconomic proposition. One tactic which helped to persuade districts to co-operate with the counties was the offer of seats on county highway committees which had a local advisory role or perhaps some executive powers.

The situation in metropolitan areas differed from that in the shires. Metropolitan counties were new organisations faced with the task of assembling resources and potential. Their districts had substantial resources and experience. So agency agreements were made and were drawn in wide terms. The counties retained responsibility for finance, strategic planning, the setting of standards and perhaps the design of major projects. Practical work stayed with the districts. The sole executive tasks retained by Merseyside were motorway maintenance and the care of the Mersey tunnels. However, in West Yorkshire the picture changes for the metropolitan county inherited the resources of the former West Riding. West Yorkshire managed to persuade all its districts except Bradford of the advantages of a unified highways service. Accordingly the districts, other than Bradford, agreed to surrender their statutory rights to maintain local urban roads in return for representation on divisional county committees that have some executive control over highway operations. The pattern was not dissimilar to arrangements in Surrey described above.[7] Between Bradford and West Yorkshire there was a head-on clash. Bradford applied to the Secretary of State for a direction that West Yorkshire must grant agency for county roads in Bradford: West Yorkshire put in a counter claim that Bradford's statutory highway duties should be exercised by the County under an agency agreement. This idea that powers should move upwards to the top tier as a result of ministerial intervention was unique and perhaps cheeky. Not surprisingly, the official ruling was to accept neither claim, so Bradford and West Yorkshire carry out their responsibilities in accordance with the basic division of highway powers decreed by the 1972 Act. However, the DOE letter of decision regretted that these authorities had not been able to agree to work through a single highways organisation.

The split in highway powers is likely to be a source of future trouble. In 1979, when most agency agreements terminate, many counties may refuse to renew them in the interests of unified and more efficient administration. Such a policy would lead to district protests and strained relations between the two tiers.

Both counties and districts have powers in relationship to bridleways and footpaths. They can make agreements with landowners to dedicate routes to the public. Subject to the agreement of the Secretary of State they can make orders to create new routes. *Prima facie* this duplication of powers seems unnecessary; but it may, in this particular case, help to stimulate action.

Libraries
The reduction in the number of library authorities caused by the 1972 Act was larger than that for any other local government service. Before the changeover there were 321 library authorities in the English provinces; afterwards there were only 76, i.e. the shire counties, the metropolitan districts and the Isles of Scilly. Public libraries had developed during the nineteenth century on the basis of independent and often small urban units. Rural areas lagged behind. County councils did not obtain library powers until 1919 and counties provided a service in those areas not already covered. Subsequently some of the smaller borough and urban district libraries were absorbed into the county system. The Public Libraries Act 1964 authorised, but did not require, the issue of

ministerial Orders enforcing the amalgamation of a library serving fewer than 40,000 people with the county service. But in 1972 many medium-sized towns, some below 40,000, still had separate libraries. Thus the process of integration was more complex than that for functions previously organised on a county council and county borough basis. To take Hampshire as an example, besides the county borough libraries of Portsmouth and Southampton the non-county boroughs of Aldershot, Andover, Gosport and Winchester each had their own libraries that had to be brought together into a unified county organisation. Even shires which suffered no boundary changes and contained no county boroughs could still be affected by this aspect of reorganisation. Indeed, the Isle of Wight was the only county completely unconcerned. Similarly, almost all the metropolitan districts had to make some adjustments. Yet the metropolitan areas were relatively homogenous in character; they were less affected than the shires by the problem of blending the different needs and methods of provision for diverse urban and rural areas.

For the public the most immediate benefit of reorganisation was that readers living on the fringes of large towns became entitled to use the library in the urban centre without payment of a fee. The counties had developed a system based largely on small branches and mobile libraries that move round the more remote rural areas. Urban libraries had done more to develop specialised collections and a reference service. The DES Circular 5/73 on library reorganisation stressed the advantages of integrating bookstocks, the prospect that larger library units could afford to employ more specialised staff and the need for more specialised staff training. The Circular also emphasised the desirability of extending the range of exhibitions and displays associated with the library service. It suggested that additional accommodation for cultural activities might be obtained in 'buildings no longer needed for civic purposes as a result of reorganisation'.

The task of bringing together county and urban systems raised a variety of delicate administrative and political issues. Because a county library has been largely an organisation for circulating books round branches, often from rather shabby headquarters premises, it has not in the past commanded the same degree of public support as the more unified and imposing urban libraries. The latter usually formed a separate department of the local authority. In counties the library usually constituted a sub-section of the education department and, some would say, tended to be dwarfed by it. The pattern has become less uniform. Many county libraries are separated from the education department and the county librarian has become a chief officer of second-rank status, i.e. he does not serve on the management team. Nor is there a separate Library Committee. A majority of county libraries are now governed through a Leisure and Recreation Committee (the precise title varies) rather than by the Education Committee. Whether this divorce from education is advantageous is a matter for argument. Certainly it is a little embarrassing to the DES, for a large part of the case for insisting that libraries must be a top-tier function in shire counties rested on the importance of keeping close links between the libraries and the education service.

The other main argument in favour of larger library organisations was that bigger and integrated bookstocks could be more efficiently used and would provide a better service. Yet some former library authorities were divided by reorganisation. Where a district was moved from one shire to another the effect was trivial. But where part of a shire was taken into a metropolitan area, responsibility for the library service moved down from the top-tier to second-tier level. In accordance with the general rules governing the transfer of property an appropriate fraction of the county bookstocks was transferred to the metropolitan districts, each of which contained one or more of the former urban library authorities. In the case of material used by the general reader this reallocation was not of importance. To split up a specialised collection is more serious. The county libraries had relatively few specialised collections but the former West Riding had developed a very fine service of assistance to teachers based on the county headquarters at Wakefield. Had the resources that supported this facility been distributed among the new library authorities in the former West Riding area, the service would have been shattered. So it was agreed that the facilities be managed as a whole by the Wakefield Metropolitan District and that the neighbouring authorities continue to use the service and contribute financially towards it.

Reorganisation of the library system was aggravated and delayed by discussions on the possible use of agency. The general DOE Circular on agency had suggested that libraries might offer scope for this type of county/district co-operation. The DOE had to find openings for the application of agency provisions in the 1972 Act and one suspects that there was inter-departmental pressure on the DES to admit the use of agency in the library service. In addition, the extinction of so many urban libraries was likely to arouse strong local pressure for some measure of decentralisation in the new arrangements. In fact, the scope for decision by elected representatives in relation to detailed administration is limited; *a fortiori* the scope for agency must be limited also. The crucial decision—how much to spend—must be a matter for the Policy and Resources Committee of the library authority. Book selection is a matter for professional judgement. Indeed, local libraries agree to concentrate non-fiction purchases on particular subjects; these decisions are made not by councillors but by librarians working together on a regional basis. Rural areas are served by travelling libraries. The optimum area for the operation of these vehicles can rarely coincide with district boundaries, so it is difficult to see how their control could be subject to an agency agreement.

DES Circular 5/73 suggested in detail how agency might be used. One idea was that a district might participate in the selection of library staff: however, this was contrary to the tradition of the county library service where staff selection below the level of the chief librarian and his deputy had been decided by officers. The Circular indicated that within the county determination of the budget and general strategy of development, the following items might be the subject of local agency arrangements: (i) supervision of day-to-day management, including decisions on hours of opening; (ii) the provision of supplementary material to reflect local needs and interests; (iii) the purchase of furniture and equipment; (iv) maintenance of library buildings and grounds; (v) enforcement of library bye-laws; and (vi) development of co-operation between the library service and local societies to promote cultural activities. This list demonstrates that the scope for district participation must be restricted. Item (i) must be constrained by the provision in the county budget for staff establishment. Item (iii) is open to the criticism that county library headquarters should be better informed than district councillors about the availability, suitability and comparative cost of library furniture, quite apart from the prospect of economies achieved from county-wide bulk purchase. Item (vi) is partly the promotion of good relationships rather than questions for executive decision.

Nevertheless, the vast scale of library amalgamations, and the substantial local interest and, indeed, pride in local libraries made it likely that many district councils would try to retain some voice in the management of the service. Nine counties agreed to give restricted agency powers to some or all of their districts. Fifty-nine districts applied to the DES for directions that they should receive agency powers: thirty were 'holding' applications designed to stake a claim while local negotiations proceeded and twenty-nine were 'firm' applications. Ultimately, thirty-six applications were withdrawn as a result of further local discussion and twenty-three remained for ministerial decision. In no case did the Secretary of State direct a county to grant agency powers. There were perhaps two main reasons for this outcome. One was a reluctance to give mandatory instructions to local authorities. Parliament had given library powers to the shire counties so, unless an overwhelming case could be made to the contrary, the shires should decide how to run their own libraries. The second point is that the districts which had the strongest claim to agency in terms of their resources and experience were so important and central to the counties that the county services would have been seriously weakened if these powerful districts had been allowed to stand apart. This situation arose particularly in Brighton, Bristol and Hull: the reference library facilities of East Sussex, Avon and Humberside would have been seriously fragmented without the full integration of these districts.

Although the DES gave no directions about agency it did play an active role in attempting to promote harmony between counties and districts. The number of agency applications withdrawn is some measure of the success of this mediation. Some districts obtained partial satisfaction from the establishment of an advisory committee. Humberside divided itself into library areas: each area has a local library committee which contains a strong element of district representation and also exercises some delegated powers. As one of these library areas is coterminous with Hull, the City can still play a part in making library policy.

There is no doubt that professional library staff are broadly hostile to the concept of agency because they do not feel that district councils can do much to assist in the management of their service. Where agency has been adopted, it has been accepted largely for 'political' reasons—to promote happier relationships with district councillors. The exercise may well go sour if district committees come to feel frustrated by lack of scope for taking decisions. On the other hand, librarians are fully aware of the value of public interest and support. Pressure from district councils for better facilities can be of great assistance, especially since the public library is sometimes thought of as a Cinderella, waiting at the end of the queue for additional capital and current expenditure.

Passenger Transport

Metropolitan counties, shire counties and non-metropolitan districts each have quite different functions in relation to passenger transport under the Local Government Act 1972. It is convenient to discuss them in reverse order. Where a non-metropolitan district contains an authority that had operated a public transport system, then the district continues to provide the service. The district undertaking has to be run in conformity with the strategic transport policy of the shire county but a district can charge a county with any loss caused by following county instructions.

For the shire counties the concern with passenger transport is almost a new responsibility.[8] Their task is to promote an adequate public service by road and rail through co-operation with British Rail and the various bus operators, public and private, within the county. Unconventional means of transport may be encouraged in sparsely populated areas. The pattern of services has to be considered in relation to long-term planning of land use. Counties and non-metropolitan districts can subsidise uneconomic services or concessionary fares which meet an important public need. So for the shires there are two related aspects of the transport function. One is a specialised aspect of strategic planning; the other, subsidies, requires experience of transport operation and economics.

Shire counties had not previously employed experts in transport. Nor was it possible for all shires to recruit such officers for they were not available in the required numbers. The solution offered by DOE Circular 5/73 was for the shires to appoint as part-time advisers people with senior management experience in bus operation, including the staff of district undertakings. The difficulty is that a major part of the authority's responsibility is to negotiate over how much money is needed to maintain services that would otherwise collapse. Part-time advisers cannot always be used for this purpose owing to the probable conflict of interest. As far as the shires are concerned the problem of coping with their public transport responsibilities does not stem from reconstruction as such; rather is it an example of the problem of making arrangements to cope with fresh responsibilities.

A metropolitan county is a Passenger Transport Authority (PTA). So in addition to a co-ordinating role they themselves provide road services through a Passenger Transport Executive. PTEs were established under the Transport Act 1968 for Tyneside, the West Midlands and the north-west conurbations as a new form of transport management board which had similarities to the type of public corporation used by the post-war Labour Government to administer nationalised industries. These Executives were composed of full-time officers and had considerable commercial freedom. However, they were responsible to Passenger Transport Authorities, consisting of persons nominated by local authorities in the area, for their estimates and main policy proposals. Under the Local Government

Act 1972 these Passenger Transport Authorities disappeared and their duties were allocated to the metropolitan counties. Indeed, a county has wider powers of control than the former PTAs. It can give directions to the Executive, review its organisation and require information to be provided on operations, expenditure and accounts. But a metropolitan county cannot over-ride the professional judgement of its Executive without regard to the financial consequences. Thus if the county requires the provision of a service that the Executive judges to be uneconomic, the county must agree to make good the financial loss from its own revenues.

An early task for metropolitan bus undertakings was to design a livery for their vehicles. It was thought that a new livery would have a valuable public relations impact in helping to promote general recognition and acceptance of the metropolitan counties.

The impact of the 1972 Act on metropolitan areas was not uniform. Greater Manchester, Merseyside, Tyne and Wear and the West Midlands inherited organisations which, although of recent origin, were firmly established. Some minor boundary adjustments were required; e.g. when Greater Manchester took over the SELNEC PTA, Wigan had to be added to the system; and Merseyside incorporated the Southport municipal service. Certainly the four counties with established PTEs had to review policy but they could do so from the basis of assembled and operating resources. South and West Yorkshire each had the far greater task of creating PTEs which would take over and unify services. The Yorkshire PTEs may well become more fully integrated into county administration than the others which had earlier and more independent existence.

A change of emphasis has taken place between the Transport Act 1968 and the Local Government Act 1972. The intention in 1968 was to establish unified and efficient public undertakings that would aim at neither profit nor loss. They would be semi-independent of other public bodies. They were to operate in the public interest defined in the limited terms of passenger transport. Such a concept is quite divorced from the corporate approach to the management of public services. Under the 1972 Act the outlook is broader. Transport undertakings become one means among many to promote the public good by minimising the strains of urban life or the remoteness of rural life. So policies of bus operation are to be linked with traffic control, road construction and development control as an aspect of long-term strategic planning. The planning responsibilities are the same for all counties but in metropolitan areas the pressure of congestion is more acute. The emphasis on the social aspect of transport will increase the subsidy element both in relation to uneconomic services and to concessionary fares. Indeed, the question of the extent and nature of financial assistance for public transport is becoming a major policy issue in local government.

Planning

Town and country planning received exceptional treatment in the 1972 Local Government Act. Before reorganisation the counties and county boroughs were the planning authorities. The 1972 Act divided this responsibility between counties and districts. So while the number of authorities dealing with other local government functions decreased, the number of planning authorities rose considerably. In the English provinces the number went up from 125 to 376. Stated baldly, the figures rather over-stress the amount of decentralisation since many second-tier councils had previously exercised limited delegated powers in relation to development control. Nevertheless the multiplication of councils with planning powers was contrary to the trend of the times. Essex and Kent were extreme cases where two planning authorities were replaced by fifteen.

The division of functions between the two tiers is based on the theory that counties should undertake broad strategic planning while the districts deal with the details of development control. However, there is some overlap between the duties. The more important development applications are classed as county matters and stand to be determined by the county authority. These include proposals which are in conflict with county planning policy, items which could have effects outside a single district and anything relating to mineral working. Districts are to make local plans to fill in the details of the county's strategic plan, but in some cases the task of making the local plan may revert to the county. There are also concurrent powers for the acquisition and disposal of land, the clearance of derelict land, conservation areas, tree preservation orders, the provision of gipsy sites and the provision of country parks. This duplication leaves many opportunities for conflict and frustration.

Throughout the country the county planning officers met district representatives to frame schemes to control the administration of the service. Some of these schemes were agreed by 1 April 1974; some were not. Details of these agreements would provide material for a separate study. They had to decide how the county was to monitor district activities to ensure that county interests were preserved. Was the county to exercise its statutory right to see all planning applications? What arrangements were to be made over the use of concurrent powers and, in particular, the preparation of local plans? Should development applications which affect main highways be submitted to county engineers via the county Planning Department? Where a county grants outline permission in relation to a county matter, should the district have the right to control details of the development? An obvious cause of dispute is whether a particular application falls within the category of county matters. Some authorities have created a third category for cases intermediate between county and district matters. Counties have a reserve power to give a direction to a district as to how an application shall be determined where it 'would substantially and adversely affect their interests as local planning authority'.[9] Bad feeling is likely to develop if this power is used often.

To investigate fully the reasons why the Conservative Government decided to split up the planning process would be to go beyond the present purpose. The immediate task is to examine the consequences of the decision. Yet the reasons and the consequences are not unrelated. Ministers had been under pressure to ensure that the district authorities were given enough to do to justify the rejection of the Royal Commission proposal for unitary authorities. At the same time there was a demand for fuller public participation and consultation on local planning. Preservation of the environment became a popular cry. Planning decisions would clearly seem less remote if made by districts rather than counties. The participation element was emphasised further by giving parish councils fourteen days to comment on development applications.[10] If wider involvement in the planning process is secured, the decision made will be more sensitive to local lobbying. There may well be a greater tendency, especially in more prosperous middle-class areas, to restrain development or to attempt to improve its quality.

In the context of public participation the new system is not entirely helpful because the division of function between county and district is not easy for people to comprehend. Indeed, one wonders how many councillors would be happy to answer an examination question which required a detailed explanation of the part to be played by the various authorities concerned with the planning process.

At early meetings of the new district planning committees some hesitation was evident. Important decisions were avoided either by postponement for further consideration or by references to the county. This tendency will disappear as the committees and their staff gain more experience and confidence.

One of the main objections to the division of planning powers was the fear that districts would not be able to recruit staff of good quality to supervise development control. It was argued that greater intellectual satisfaction could be gained from the broader vistas of strategic planning. The more able staff would be attracted by the research function, the interpretation of data and the evaluation of long-term trends. So they would stay with the counties. The districts, offering work of limited scope, would be left with less ambitious and less far-sighted officers. In the event, the outcome was quite different. Third- and fourth-tier officers in county planning departments were happy to move over to the districts to become chief officers or deputies. Such a move offered a large increase in salary—of £2,000 per annum or even more. Those who became district chief officers joined the management team and so enjoyed a wider span of activity than that provided by a place within a county planning hierarchy. And a district planning officer can have a more immediate impact on events than a senior county planning officer working on long-range objectives.

The increase in the number of planning authorities greatly improved employment opportunities. There were insufficient qualified staff to fill the new establishments. Many authorities were left with vacancies. The shires suffered as their staff moved away to the districts. The situation became so serious that the Local Government Staff Commission was forced to impose a ban on national advertisements for planning staff in November 1973. The effect of this move was to limit planners to jobs offered by new authorities which occupied part of the area of their existing employers. There was some criticism of the Staff Commission's policy as being too drastic. Yet without some type of restriction the planning system might have broken down altogether. An unfortunate aspect was that the policy of the ringed fence did not have a uniform effect throughout the country. Inevitably it imposed a greater drain on those authorities that had lost territory to the metropolitan counties or to the new shires of Avon, Cleveland and Humberside. So some authorities faced much graver staff shortages than others. Among the metropolitan counties Tyne and Wear was successful in its recruitment but the West Midlands was poorly placed.

Large-scale movement of staff had a variety of consequences. Development control depends very much on knowledge of local circumstances. So a great deal of effort was required by newly appointed officials to master details of the locality. This problem was eased by the geographical restraints on recruitment: district planning officers were commonly former members of the county staff and so had prior acquaintance with the area. The well estab-

lished personal links between county and district staff also facilitated co-operation between the two tiers and meant that district
staff were well informed about county policy. It is also the case that
some district planners had relatively little experience of development control as their previous duties with the county had been
concerned with longer term strategic issues. However, this was a
transient problem to be remedied by pressure of work. Another
transient difficulty was the delay in dealing with some development
applications after reorganisation day, caused not only by transfer of
staff but also by the movement of offices and their contents.

Counties with depleted staffs will find it hard to carry out their
responsibilities. Section 183 of the 1972 Act requires counties to
prepare a development plan scheme. During 1974 progress towards
this goal was slow in many areas. Some counties even had difficulty
in giving full attention to county matters referred to them by districts. One county planning officer very highly placed in his pro-
fession suggested to me that it would be necessary to judge these
cases less on the basis of carefully prepared data but more on a
'hunch' derived from past experience. Some shires did manage to
keep together specialised teams, e.g. experts on conservation and
landscape architecture. Yet such teams can be used to full advantage only if consulted by the districts. The danger exists that districts will wish to demonstrate their independence by making separate specialist appointments. There were also districts which moved
rapidly to employ staff to make local plans when the county had not
yet produced an adequate framework within which local plans
could be properly prepared.

The twin problems of staff shortage and division of responsibility
can be eased by maximum co-operation between counties and districts. Yet this is not easy to achieve. Originally the Government
had proposed a unified staff structure serving both a county and its
districts:[11] the idea was dropped owing to hostility from the districts. The attempt in Somerset to create a unified planning service
has largely broken down.[12] In Durham a rather different scheme is
being operated by the county and all the districts except Durham
City and Sedgefield. Each authority retains its statutory powers but
the work is carried out by a county-wide planning staff employed by
the County Council. The six districts in the scheme make but a
single appointment, that of District Planning Officer. The county-
wide staff are divided into three sections. Some are posted to district
offices to work on district planning matters; some are at county
offices to work on county matters; the remainder are specialist staff
whose services are available wherever they are needed. This pattern

provides expert resources for the districts which otherwise they could not afford. Yet there are difficulties, e.g. the decisions on priorities in the allocation of staff time and the position of an officer serving two masters who may have conflicting interests and opposing opinions. Another complication is that the districts which stand aside suffer a financial penalty. There is no differential county rate for planning. So Durham City and Sedgefield pay the full county precept, which covers the cost of development control staff for the other districts, as well as paying separately, for their own planning staff. Arguably, this is unfair. It could also put pressure on the districts to join the county scheme. Nevertheless, the County of Durham is running a valuable experiment: the experience of its operation should repay further study.

Critics of the bifurcation of planning responsibilities are convinced that it will do grave damage to the quality of the service. The change came at a bad moment for the county authorities for they were deeply immersed in the preparation of the new-style structure plans. One planning officer suggested that the morale of county planning staff was damaged because they felt themselves no longer in full control. There was doubt about how far the districts would be effective in enforcing county policy. But any loss of morale could be for reasons unconnected with local government structure. Strategic planning must become a more frustrating occupation in a period of zero or limited growth caused by a combination of a falling birthrate and adverse national economic prospects.

The two-tier planning system must be more expensive and more cumbersome. Counties scrutinise district activities to ensure that county policies are not endangered. The result is more consultations and a bigger paperchase. For the moment the increase in cost has been checked by lack of qualified staff, but as this shortage is remedied the cost will rise. However, the success of the new system is not to be judged solely in terms of expense and speed. The non-metropolitan districts were greatly strengthened by the acquisition of planning powers and the democratic element in the process has been reinforced.

Police and Fire
The constitutional position of the police differs from that of all other local government services. Police authorities are not county councils but County Police Committees, which consist partly of magistrates. Chief Constables have more independence than other chief officers because of the need for impartiality in law enforce-

ment. And many counties were, and still are, merged for police purposes because of the operational requirement for large areas. Police reform preceded the wider reform of local administration because a substantial reduction in the number of police forces was secured by the Police Act 1964. In 1974 the task was to make boundary adjustments to fit the new county areas rather than to plan for fewer and bigger police forces.

Police Committees are unique in local government because one-third of the members are magistrates. Councillors who serve on these bodies are selected by the same process as applies to other county committees. Magistrates are chosen by fellow magistrates. The procedure is complex, especially in the metropolitan counties. Here petty sessional divisions were reorganised in 1974 and magistrates were assigned to the new divisions. The Secretary of State made regulations to determine the number of magistrates on the Metropolitan Courts Committee for each metropolitan district. These committees then had to agree on a scheme of representation on the Joint Committee of District Magistrates Courts Committees and appoint members to the Joint Committee. This Joint Committee then had to agree a scheme for the appointment of magistrates to the County Police Committee—a scheme which needed Home Office approval. When all this procedure had been completed, the magistrates to serve on the Police Committee could be chosen. In shire counties the position is a little simpler as petty sessional divisions elect members to the Magistrates Courts Committee and the latter body elects members to the County Police Committee. Elections by magistrates are always conducted without discussion and by secret ballot. For combined forces the nominations to the police authority are made by each Magistrates Courts Committee and county council within the area. In some cases the new Magistrates Courts Committees were not organised in time to elect members to the new police authority; to circumvent the temporary difficulty the Secretary of State was given power to direct how magistrates were to be appointed until the system prescribed by statute could operate.[13]

Before 1974 the police authorities were based on counties and county boroughs, but many county borough forces had been combined with the surrounding counties. Prior to the Police Act 1964 there had been over one hundred police forces in England. By 1972 the figure was reduced to forty-one. As from 1974 it became thirty-seven. However, only seven of the thirty-seven are combined whereas prior to the 1974 reorganisation a majority had been joint forces. This simplification arises partly from the fact that the end of county borough status and the disappearance of the smaller county councils reflects the changes that had already taken place in police reorganisation. Thus the combined Derby County and Borough Police became the Derbyshire Police, and the combined force for the three separate parts of Lincolnshire became the Lincolnshire Police. The extent of the police reshuffle varied enormously. Metropolitan areas had to build wholly new organisations by welding together resources from former police authorities whereas in some shires nothing had to be altered. Where combined forces existed before 1974 county boundary adjustments within the area had no effect on the police: boundary changes between Berkshire, Buckinghamshire and Oxfordshire were irrelevant to the work of the Thames Valley force.

Counties combined for police purposes	Name of combined force
Berkshire, Buckinghamshire, Oxfordshire	Thames Valley
Devon, Cornwall	Devon and Cornwall
East Sussex, West Sussex	Sussex
Hampshire, Isle of Wight	Hampshire
Hereford and Worcester, Salop	West Mercia

Five of the seven combined forces continue, albeit with minor boundary adjustments, the pre-1974 pattern. Cornwall and the Isle of Wight, showing a vigorous spirit of separatism, both resented the continuation of joint forces but the Home Office refused to split up the established organisations. In addition the Home Office insisted on two new combinations: Avon and Somerset, and Northumberland and Tyne and Wear. The Whitehall view seemed to be that a population of at least 450,000 was needed to provide the basis of an efficient police force and, since both Northumberland and Somerset fell well below this figure, amalgamations were essential. The Northumberland/Tyne and Wear marriage is unique for it is the sole example of a shire county and a metropolitan county being joined for police purposes.

The most involved reorganisation was needed in the north-west where a massive carve-up of the Lancashire Police reduced the population it served from 3,379,000 to 1,341,000. The new police authorities for Cheshire, Cumbria, Greater Manchester, Lancashire and Merseyside were created out of the former Cheshire, Cumbria, Lancashire, Liverpool and Bootle and Manchester and Salford forces, together with part of the former West Riding constabulary. The new authorities formed a joint committee to ease the path of transition. Its tasks were to assemble vital information, identify matters of common interest separating short- and medium-term problems and to consider how best to wind up the dying organisations and redistribute their personnel, property and resources. Elsewhere the process of reconstitution was easier, and bilateral discussions between two police authorities were generally adequate. Ten constabularies were unchanged and were spared the need for any discussions: they were Bedfordshire, Cambridgeshire, Devon and Cornwall, Essex, Hertfordshire, Kent, Leicestershire, Northamptonshire, Thames Valley and Wiltshire. Some other adjustments were trivial, e.g. between Surrey and Sussex.

Agreements between police authorities governing the redistribution of their property and personnel had to be approved by the Home Secretary. Where agreement was not reached, the Home Secretary had powers to arbitrate. In the event, everything was settled locally. Negotiations were carried out between the local police hierarchies rather than between elected representatives and this eased the way to acceptable compromises. Where police boundaries were changed each officer was asked which of the forces in the area he wished to join. So subject to the overall requirement of a balanced distribution of manpower, the disposition of uniformed personnel proceeded on the basis of individual choice. Civilian staff were reallocated like other local government officers under the rules established by the Local Government Staff Commission.[14] The choice of Chief Constable was strictly controlled by the central government. Where an area was unchanged, the existing office-holder continued automatically. Where boundaries had altered the only candidates considered, unless the Home Office otherwise determined, were the Chief Constables of the forces which prior to reorganisation covered part of the territory of the new authority.

There is a tendency—perhaps an unfortunate tendency—for police to be regarded as largely divorced from the other responsibilities of local government. The role of the police authority is more limited than that of other county committees because of the independence of the Chief Constable in relation to law enforcement. So the police authority is largely concerned with financial provision. Reorganisation has affected this separation in two ways. Because police areas now coincide more often with local government areas there are fewer combined forces. This should serve to strengthen the position of police authorities since the joint bodies, containing elected representatives and magistrates from more than one county, necessarily found it difficult to establish a strong corporate personality. As the identity between police and county council is now stronger, councillors serving on the police authority may feel greater responsibility for police expenditure. On the other hand, the development of the idea of corporate management by chief officers may tend to isolate the police still further. A Chief Constable is not a member of the county management team. Thus while other chief officers become more and more used to working together, the Chief Constable stays apart and does not join them.

Under Section 197 of the 1972 Act the counties become the sole fire authorities: previously this duty had been assigned to counties and county boroughs. Section 197 also gives counties the power to create combined brigades. In fact, no joint arrangements have been made. So the reorganisation of the fire service amounted to the absorption of the county borough brigades by the counties and the adjustment of county forces to fit the new county boundaries. Schemes were revoked which formerly provided joint brigades for Reading County Borough and Berkshire and Ipswich County Borough and East Suffolk.

The bringing together of fire brigades, or parts of brigades, necessarily caused some local difficulties as each brigade had had its own system of manning and duty rosters. However, these problems were eased by local negotiation and by the prospect of the national agreement to reduce hours of duty from 56 to 48 as from November 1974. So it became reasonable to continue the practice of each station until November when new arrangements had to come into force. More troublesome in some cases was the unification of control rooms and the closing of some of the existing centres. To transfer to the new county headquarters was inconvenient for some firewomen working on telecommunications. Thus in Lincolnshire, where four control rooms were due to be merged, there was a prospect of hardship and a need to use the general provisions for compensation. Again, the problems were eased because these events were not sudden. Telecommunications cannot be reorganised overnight. So there was time for staff to adjust to a new situation.

Refuse

The task of dealing with refuse was also split between the two tiers of authorities by the 1972 Act. Districts collect unwanted matter; counties dispose of it. Previously refuse had been wholly a district concern as part of their responsibility for environmental health.

Local standards of rubbish collection can vary in relation to frequency, method and the provision of dustbins. The last item can be curiously complex. Occupiers may be required to provide their own dustbins; alternatively, the local authority may provide them with or without charge. The position can depend on local legislation. Wirral Metropolitan District inherited four separate dustbin schemes connected with three local Acts.

However, the crucial issue over refuse was the transfer of disposal to the counties. This was made necessary by the need to utilise more sophisticated techniques of destruction and to promote the recycling of material. The districts sternly contested the change but they were over-ruled.[15] For many of them the cost and capacity of modern incinerators are too great. And while the aim is to reduce tipping, the distribution of tipping sites is not necessarily convenient in relation to district boundaries.

Allocation to the counties of formal responsibility for refuse disposal involves forward planning. In the immediate aftermath of April 1974 the task remained generally with the districts under the cover of agency arrangements. Disposal staff continued to be employed by the districts and the work proceeds as before until the counties are ready to take over executive control. Meanwhile the counties appointed senior staff to plan future policy; this process was hampered by a shortage of applicants with suitable qualifications and experience. The need was to acquire fresh tipping sites and more modern equipment—developments which require close consultation with planning departments. New methods of handling waste material are being encouraged by fresh legislation. The Protection of the Environment Bill, which was to give additional powers to local authorities, was lost when Parliament was dissolved for the general election in February 1974. A revised version of this measure entitled the Control of Pollution Bill became law a few months later and required disposal authorities to give comprehensive attention to the reclamation of waste materials.

DOE Circular 131/72, in discussing agency arrangements for refuse disposal, stressed that 'it would be best if such arrangements were short term until the future and overall responsibilities of the service can be clearly seen'. As a result these agreements are often of shorter duration than those for highways. Many districts will not be sorry to lose this particular function; indeed some counties took immediate control in April 1974 partly because of lack of district enthusiasm. There is increasing public interest in the recycling of waste matter and local public indignation at the unpleasant consequences of some disposal processes. But the routine administration of the service does not stir great excitement among district councillors. In this situation agency is used simply as a means of smoothing out difficulties of transition and will be temporary.

It is a matter of doubt whether the division of duty between refuse collection and disposal will help or hinder the reclamation of waste material. Districts are under growing pressure to make separate collections but may be unwilling to do so because of labour shortage. Counties could encourage more extensive action by making payments to the districts for certain materials in the way that the GLC now pays London boroughs for waste paper. But in the particular case of waste paper the Control of Pollution Act 1974 permits the districts themselves to dispose of, i.e. sell, whatever they collect.

Social Services

Social services are undergoing a period of virtually continuous change and development. In these circumstances the effect of the 1972 Act cannot be assessed in isolation. The number of local authorities responsible was reduced in exactly the same way as the number of local education authorities. The special problems of the three metropolitan districts that contain no former county boroughs applied equally to education and the social services.[16]

The Local Authority Social Services Act 1970 had started the transformation. Other developments commenced after April 1974 as a result of the National Health Service Reorganisation Act 1973 which required the establishment of joint consultative committees nominated by the health and social services authorities to ensure that their functions were complementary and fully co-ordinated. This Act also required these authorities to make their resources available for each other. However, the 1970 legislation was of greater importance. It did not confer major new powers on local councils nor did it redistribute powers. The central purpose was to bring together in a single local authority department a miscellany of activities which had grown in a piecemeal manner in separate departments. Some staff had found this process painful: they felt themselves to have lost a degree of independence in a larger organisation where their own professional expertise appeared to carry less weight.

As soon as the departments born of the 1970 Act began to settle down, the Secretary of State asked for the preparation of ten-year plans which would chart the course for future growth. An early task for the new authorities created by the 1972 Act was to review and collate these plans. It was a most valuable exercise as it demonstrated vividly the uneven level of provision that existed. Some of the former councils had spent more freely than others, but many of the disparities resulted from differing emphases and priorities. Some authorities had given most attention to services for the elderly; others had concentrated on the mentally handicapped or the physically handicapped; others had given priority to child care. Social services differ from other local government responsibilities in that the extent of the provision made is so variable. Specialised facilities may be non-existent in particular parts of the country.

In one sense responsibility for the situation is due to the patchy growth of statutory provisions. In a more profound sense the cause lies with the late recognition of the need for social services as compared with education or housing. A major task of social service departments is still to discover and decide where their help is most urgently required. There may be a tendency among some officials to avoid looking too closely under the stones lest needs are discovered that cannot be met due to lack of resources or lack of political will. The DHSS laid down guidelines governing the desirable extent of various types of welfare facilities in 1972 when the local authorities were asked to draw up their ten-year plans. These guidelines projected standards far in excess of most local authorities' provisions. To attain these standards, even over a ten-year period, will be highly expensive. Yet it is towards these goals that local councils are expected to aim.

Social services departments must provide for easy accessibility by the public and also keep in close touch with voluntary welfare organisations. The remoteness that arises from larger units of organisation must be resisted sternly. Decentralised administration is essential. In accordance with the Seebohm recommendation,[17] area offices with teams of social workers are established with complete authority to make decisions on individual clients. Headquarters staff of a social services department are concerned with broad policy issues, financial control and forward planning. In Hampshire there was felt to be a need for an intermediate layer of organisation between policy development at the centre and the office base of social workers in the field. The emphasis on decentralisation doubtless eased the unification of formerly separate units. Thus the social services department of an ex-county borough could continue with its case work unmolested.

Again in accordance with Seebohm recommendations, the appointment by local authorities of the Directors of Social Services was subject to ministerial approval.[18] Through its regional social work advisers the DHSS can assess the quality of local administrators. The extent of central influence cannot be measured by the occasions when ministerial ratification is withheld because there may be other times when it is quietly intimated to the appointing commitee that X is not acceptable or is not viewed with great favour. The implications are pernicious. If the official grapevine picks up the idea that a particular officer is 'awkward' his promotion to the top could be blocked. If ambitious men become aware of this prospect they may tend to become subservient to central influence.

This control was first introduced in 1970. The justification in the eyes of central government was the fear that local councils might make weak appointments, perhaps being unduly favourable to long-serving members of their own staff. No doubt the task of unifying what had been sections of separate departments required great skill. Also, since the concept of a Director of Social Services was new in 1970, there was no ready-made cadre of people from which to select. So there was a good opportunity for making poor choices. The 1974 reorganisation offered another chance to shunt gently aside those chief officers below top quality. Now that a new career structure has been firmly established the need for ministerial ratification of these appointments might be re-examined.

A vast majority of the new social services authorities embraced more than one of the outgoing councils with parallel responsibilities. Accordingly, they had to take some steps to equalise the standards applied by their predecessors. There were three main aspects to this task. A more uniform set of staffing establishments was required. Methods of assessment of individual needs and charges had to be standardised. Above all, there was a need to equalise levels of provision throughout an authority's domain.

The first category involves internal administration that does not affect the public directly. The management of old people's homes provides one example. They can be run in quite different ways. One system is for a superintendent to have overall charge while a matron is responsible for the personal welfare of the inmates. Alternatively, a matron can be in overall command while many administrative duties are undertaken by middle-grade staff in the local council office. The latter arrangement may have been more suitable for county boroughs where the office was closer to hand. Another example of variations in staffing establishments is in the ratio between social workers and the clerical supporting staff.

The second group of problems affects individuals directly and required the most immediate action. It is not possible to justify differing methods of charging for home helps or meals on wheels within one local authority. Often a problem was solved by adoption of the most generous of the conflicting standards. The result was to increase cost without extending the service provided: in a period of financial stringency, this generosity could have the effect of inhibiting future developments. There were instances where the outgoing authorities softened their means-testing arrangements shortly before reorganisation and so greatly increased the cost of creating equality. Not all the diverse charges were made uniform on 1 April 1974. One Director of Social Services faced with charges for meals on wheels that varied between 4p and 12p had still not made up his mind some months later on what recommendation to make to his committee. The matter was felt to be explosive because it was both simple and emotive: it is far more difficult to handle smoothly an issue that everyone can understand.

The third and most major category of problems arose from the uneven provision of facilities. In some measure this was due to basic policy differences between the former authorities. Southampton had subsidised holidays for the elderly; Hampshire had not. But for the most part the differences were the result of variations of emphasis rather than diametrically opposed decisions. And where these variations can be ironed out only by capital expenditure, the effects will be with us for years to come. Some adjustments can be made by making specialised resources available to a wider catchment area. Where a county borough had made much better *per capita* provision for the mentally handicapped than the surrounding county, its facilities can now be used to serve the whole of the new county area. Yet such an arrangement must lead to some deprivation for the less urgent cases in the former county borough area. Sharing must produce a mixture of benefit and loss wherever it takes place. In local government the effects of sharing may be greatest in the case of social services for it is here that pre-1974 standards were most disparate.

NOTES

1. It is also a matter of controversy. Some professional officers prefer the title 'trading standards' in order to stress their neutrality between consumers and traders. The Bains Report used the title 'consumer protection' and this has been generally adopted owing to its greater public and political appeal.
2. At Tameside there has been a curious historical cycle. The education office is housed in the Town Hall of the former Borough of Dukinfield. Engraved in Victorian-style lettering in the windows of a room used by the department are the words SCHOOL BOARD. Clearly the room had been used by the local School Board before 1902. Primary education then passed to the Borough before being lost to Cheshire in 1944. Thirty years later Dukinfield again became the base of an education authority but this time with comprehensive powers.
3. The issue of the status of education is directly linked with the dispute about the future of the Association of Education Committees, see pp. 175–8 *infra*.
4. For an account of the position in Somerset see P. Day, 'Agency Arrange-

ments for Highways' in *Public Finance and Accountancy* (June 1974), pp. 201–4.
5. 1970, HMSO, Ch. 12. The Report favoured a minimum population of 200,000 for highway authorities: it argued that those below 100,000 were markedly less competent.
6. After vigorous negotiations Dorset reached agreement with its districts over highway agency, save over road safety. It was accepted that road safety be included but there was a dispute with Poole over whether road safety officers should be employed by the District or the County. In the past Poole had made more extensive provision for road safety and the issue was whether it should continue to enjoy a higher standard of service than the rest of the County. The dispute was referred to the DOE and settled in favour of the County.
7. See p. 87 *supra.*
8. The Transport Act 1968 gave counties the power to subsidise uneconomic passenger services.
9. Local Government Act 1972, 16th Schedule, para. 19.
10. This had a stimulating effect on parish councils which used their new powers. Parish business increased and it became convenient to timetable meetings in relation to those of district planning committees. However, parish councils have no right to see a copy of the development applications on which their comments are invited!
11. White Paper on *Local Government in England. Government Proposals for Reorganisation,* February 1971, Cmnd 4584, para. 21.
12. See pp. 86–7 *supra.*
13. The Police (Appointment of Police Authorities and Chief Constables) Order, SI 734 of 1973, Article 4.
14. See Ch. 6 *infra.*
15. An amendment restoring refuse disposal to non-metropolitan districts was carried on the Report Stage of the Local Government Bill by a majority of four. But ministers stuck to their policy and with the assistance of the House of Lords the amendment was subsequently reversed. See HC Deb., Vol. 841, cols 717–54 and Vol. 843, cols 1096–126; also HL Deb., Vol. 335, cols 876–900. Some districts had already developed joint disposal arrangements before 1972.
16. See p. 98 *supra.*
17. *Report of the Committee on Local Authority and Allied Personal Social Services,* Ch. XIX, 1967–8, Cmnd 3703, xxxii.
18. *Ibid.,* paras 663–6 and Local Government Act 1972, S. 112 (4) (g).

Chapter 6

STAFF

The Local Government Staff Commission
The reshaping of local authorities involved a massive reshuffle of
staff. It created a substantial human problem. Some officers feared
redundancy; others faced early retirement; others were worried
about career prospects; others were concerned about the inconvenience of a change in job location. The total effect could have
been seriously damaging to staff morale and could have produced
added difficulties in the transition period. However, the atmosphere
created by reorganisation was not one of unallayed pessimism.
Many staff felt that the new system would provide brighter
opportunities, that conditions of work in larger organisations would
be more satisfactory. Whether the prospect of change is stimulating
or depressing depends on the outlook of the individual and his
personal situation. The restless and ambitious souls welcome the
opportunity for movement; the comfortable and the weary resent
the stress caused by disturbance. Full employment also reduced
worries. A young office worker could readily move to a job outside
local government. Older staff, without many formal qualifications
but with much experience of the routine of local administration,
faced greater difficulties; for them a move would mean loss of
seniority in an unknown environment in which their past experience
would be of less value. The staff of smaller councils being amalgamated with larger authorities probably feared they would lose in the
competition within the larger unit.[1] Administrative staff in education and social service departments of former county boroughs
faced a similar situation.

The Institute of Local Government at Birmingham undertook a
survey of staff attitudes to reorganisation in 1973 before job
prospects under the new regime had become clear.[2] The results
showed that staff of rural districts were most pessimistic about the
future. The most optimistic groups were the most highly paid, the
best qualified, the young and those with the shorter periods of service either in local government as a whole or with their present

authority. The ambitious in local government are used to changing from one employer to another and welcomed reorganisation as another opportunity to move on and move up. There were some variations in attitudes between departments. Least hopeful were the planners, perhaps because the division of the planning function between counties and districts created maximum uncertainty. Most hopeful were the librarians, perhaps because their workplaces were separated from other departments and so they were less exposed to the gloom of corridor gossip.

In spite of the tendency of rumour to aggravate anxiety, it became clear that the majority of clerical staff—the lower paid—would not be greatly affected. The manual workers remained unconcerned by the discussions on reorganisation. Many of them would be moved from one authority to another but the general nature of their duties was not to alter and there was no immediate threat to job prospects. The dust cart would still go round the streets even if there were a fresh emblem on its door. It was anticipated that there might be changes in working conditions, e.g. where a depot was closed, but these local difficulties could be managed within the normal process of industrial negotiations. The attention of the main union, the National Union of Public Employees, was concentrated on the new health and water authorities which were felt to constitute a greater threat to the interests of the membership. The Union appreciated that the new and larger local authorities would seek to streamline working practices and might use their greater financial resources to introduce more labour-saving machinery. Such a policy could lead to redundancy unless either there was a widespread labour shortage or, alternatively, unless local authorities improved their standard of service. But in 1973 and 1974 these were not urgent questions. Rather were they issues likely to arise after the new councils had settled in and had time to review their inheritance. In particular, moves towards rationalisation were expected as agency arrangements relating to highways and refuse disposal were amended or brought to an end.

To return to the administrative, professional and clerical staff, the extent of change varied from place to place. For a shire county left with an unaltered boundary but which perhaps absorbed a small or medium sized county borough, the effect on most of the county staff was small. For the staff of a rural district centred on a small town that was certain not to become the headquarters of the new district, reorganisation implied that the office might close completely. Elsewhere the departments of the same authority could be affected differently; the administrative and office staffs of the education and

E

social service departments of county boroughs faced redeployment, but other departments, e.g. housing, were unaffected. In other places there was uncertainty. Where the geographical area of an authority was to be divided, how would its staff be divided? There was also uncertainty about procedural matters. How would the new authorities go about the task of appointing staff? Would they follow similar rules? What compensation would be available for those who suffered financial loss through moving from one post to another? The Government appreciated the anxieties that would arise. The initial White Paper published by the Conservative Government in February 1971 announced the intention to establish a Staff Commission to advise on the recruitment and transfer of personnel and the safeguarding of staff interests.[3] Subsequently a consultation paper from the DOE invited suggestions for matters on which fuller discussion was desirable. NALGO was particularly insistent on the need for a Staff Commission as it felt that such a body could protect its members from a local council that acted unfairly to staff. NALGO suggested eleven items for fuller consideration.[4]

1. The personnel and functions of the Staff Commission.
2. The need for regional machinery or panels of the Staff Commission.
3. The method of appointment of chief officers to the new authorities.
4. Limitations on recruitment to ensure that senior posts are allocated to officers already in the local government service.
5. Retraining of staffs for whom comparable posts are not available in the new authorities.
6. Disturbance allowances.
7. The importance of local authorities arranging joint consultation with staff on all aspects of reorganisation.
8. The early announcement by new authorities of their administrative centres.
9. Review of superannuation and related matters.
10. Revised and improved compensation provisions.
11. The Staff Commission to establish machinery for the provision of information on the number of staff required and available to the new authorities.

Further action was taken on most of these matters. Staff consultation (no. 7) was considered above.[5] No. 5 proved not to be a serious problem. No. 11 implied the framing of a national manpower budget for local government but this was impossible in the transition period as the new establishments could not be finalised until the new authorities had agreed upon their staffing requirements. No. 8 aimed at securing information about job location, but it tended to oversimplify the problem as many authorities were forced to operate from more than one centre due to accommodation problems.

Section 257 of the Local Government Act 1972 duly authorised the Secretary of State to appoint a Local Government Staff Commission. In fact, it was established before the Bill became law and in the interim period was known as the Local Government Staff Advisory Committee. According to the Act the task of the Commission was to keep under review the arrangements for the recruitment of staff by the new authorities and for transfers of staff between the old authorities and the new. Further, the Commission was to consider staffing problems caused by the reorganisation and to advise the Secretary of State on any steps necessary to safeguard the interests of staff. Eight regional offices dealt with the individual problems of local authorities while the headquarters in London concentrated on general policy. The Commission worked on similar lines to the parallel body used in the London reorganisation nine years earlier. Essentially its task was to encourage, advise and warn. It was to respect the independence and legitimate rights of the new councils so it had no power to make appointments nor did it seek to influence the appointments made. It had no jurisdiction over pay, grading or compensation. All this followed the London model.[6] Local authorities were broadly content with this situation as it offered a prospect of minimum interference by the Commission. NALGO would have preferred the Commission to have had a rather wider ambit of activity.

In practice the role of the Commission was more vigorous than one might expect from the wording of the Act. The distinction between power and authority in British public administration is becoming increasingly marked. The Staff Commission is an excellent example of this trend. The word power is used here in the sense of being able to force others to accept your authority either by law or by *force majeure:* the word authority is used to mean the ability to get others to accept your will. The Staff Commission exercised an authority over local councils that was unchallenged. Yet it had no power of its own. Any sanction it could impose was indirect. Subsection 2 of Section 257 enabled the Secretary of State to issue directions to a local authority in relation to the implementation of advice received from the Staff Commission. This 'birch in the cupboard' technique proved effective and no such directions were required.

At an early stage the Staff Commission (then the Advisory Committee) received strong representations on many of the matters noted above which had already been pressed on the DOE. In particular NALGO sought to safeguard the interests of its members by imposing restraints on staff appointments. It wanted a ban on recruitment from outside the local government service during the period of reorganisation except for some junior staff and trainees for certain professions.[7] Such action would have been beyond the power of the Commission. However, in its first Circular the Commission urged local authorities not to make appointments which might increase the risk of local redundancies. Vacancies in senior posts might be postponed by retaining officers beyond normal retiring age; vacancies might be covered by arranging for officers to perform a dual role; appointments could be made on an acting basis; applications might be restricted to officers already serving in the area of the county or district[8] A later Circular from the Commission, LGSC 6/72, identified two main objectives in addition to protecting staff interests. The public should be protected by 'facilitating the smooth and efficient introduction of the new system'. Second, the new authorities should make their senior appointments without delay. There was no insistence from the Commission on the need to find the best candidate for each job: rather the emphasis was on 'avoiding undue disturbance' of staff.

The concept of geographical restriction on who could apply for a particular post was subsequently developed and became a major feature of the Commission's work. It advised the new councils that applications should, in the first instance, be restricted to officers serving within the recruitment areas shown below.

LIMITATION ON RECRUITMENT

Type of authority	Chief executives	Chief officers	Other posts
Counties	England and Wales (excluding London)	New county[9]	New county
Metropolitan districts	England and Wales (excluding London)	New county[9]	New district
Non-metropolitan districts	New county	New county	New district

This advice was accepted by the new councils although minor

modifications to the pattern were agreed where the nature of boundary changes caused particular anomalies. The restraint had multiple effects. It simplified appointment procedures by reducing competition. It reduced the cost of arranging interviews and the amount of moving between different parts of the country. It helped to stress the difference in status between Chief Executives of the major authorities and all other local government officers. It aided anticipation of who might be appointed to a particular post and thereby minimised personal anxiety and expectations. It ensured that a high proportion of new appointees would have local knowledge. It isolated London from the reorganisation.

Restricted competition did have disadvantages. Fewer fresh faces produce fewer new ideas. But in the general upheaval perhaps new ideas were less necessary than usual. More serious was the possibility that restricted competition would produce a short list without a first class candidate for a particular senior post. This prospect was strengthened because so many chief officers and deputies took the option of early retirement.[10] And where a council was a little slow in making appointments, the best candidates on the short list might have obtained jobs elsewhere.[11] Faced with the lack of a good candidate for a senior post, an appointing committee had two choices—make an appointment that was felt to be less than wholly satisfactory or apply to the Staff Commission for consent to widen the catchment area. The second alternative involved delay and did not necessarily produce superior candidates.

There were two parts to the wider advertisement procedure. The first was to open a post to all local government officers in England and Wales outside London. Local authorities were expected to consult with staff representatives before seeking permission for this step from the regional office of the Staff Commission. Consent was withheld infrequently, usually where a professional skill was in short supply and a particular authority already had a reasonable share of the available talent. The second step was to extend the catchment area to London and to people outside the local government service. (For Chief Executives of counties and metropolitan districts this was the only possible move.) At this level consent had to be sought from Staff Commission headquarters and was not so readily obtained. There was resistance from NALGO to appointments from outside the local government service. And there was a general fear that were applicants allowed from London, then the metropolis would suffer a serious loss of experienced officials attracted by the conditions of life, including cheaper accommodation, in the provinces. Restrictions on recruitment were lifted finally in July 1974 in spite of objections from the London Boroughs Association.

The main burden of administering these restrictions had fallen on the eight part-time Assistant Commissioners who controlled the regional offices and also kept in personal touch with local authorities in their area. All the eight were former local government officials of high rank; no doubt, they were selected for their personal qualities and ability to command the confidence of staff. Their work involved some consideration of the calibre of individuals, because the question of whether wider advertisement of a job should be permitted depended upon an assessment of the quality of candidates within the local ringed fence. It was difficult for an Assistant Commissioner to refuse a determined request for wider advertisement since this could be tantamount to pressing a shadow council to choose a local applicant felt to be less than fully satisfactory. Most authorities were quite willing to appoint local people well known to them. Just occasionally there was a desire to seek wider pastures due to a local personality clash or a desire to start the new organisation with new faces, perhaps linked with the Petula Clark theme that 'the other man's grass is always greener'.

NALGO gave heavy emphasis to the need for free and fair competition for posts within the geographical restrictions. Often there was an obvious candidate for a top job. Where two or more authorities were amalgamated and one was substantially larger than the other it tended to form the core of the new council. The chief officers of the core authority would be more highly paid, probably be better qualified and have wider experience. They were the probable choices for the new chief officer posts. However, appointments were almost always made after a due process of formal application, short listing and competitive interview, even where the outcome was a foregone conclusion. An element of charade entered some of these proceedings but they served to satisfy the principle that justice shall be seen to be done.[12] In a few cases chief officers were appointed without the formality of interview. This had the advantage of saving time and so speeded up the process of creating the administrative framework for a new authority. The Town Clerk of Bradford was nominated as Chief Executive of the Bradford metropolitan district at the inaugural meeting of the new council.

Transfer to new authorities
The competitive process applied to the more senior administrative and professional posts. For the top two, three or four levels, committees of councillors conducted interviews. For intermediate levels

interviewing was done by chief officers. More junior posts were distributed on the basis of a straight transfer from an old authority to a new one. This transfer system also applied to all teaching staff and all outdoor and manual workers. For the vast majority of employees the reorganisation made no difference to the sort of work they had to do. But for some office workers there was a move from one building to another and this could involve a move from one town to another. These changes were spread over time and certainly did not all take place on 1 April 1974. Nevertheless they were bound to cause difficulty and hardship in some cases. The Government was careful to consult interested organisations on how the redistribution of jobs should be organised and a consultation paper was issued in March 1973. After considering the views of staff associations the DOE issued Circular 101/73 together with a related Memorandum which explained how the transfers were to be carried out.[13]

The basis of the system was that employment should follow function. Thus if responsibility for housing were moved from rural district A to district council B then the housing staff of authority A were simply handed over to authority B. The vast majority of employees could be dealt with by this formula. However, there were problem areas. An obvious example is the physical division of a former authority, as in Somerset where a large part of the historic shire was allocated to the new county of Avon. Here the local authorities had to make local transfer schemes to share the staff between them. The staff were consulted to see where they would prefer to work. The actual reallocation was then made based on the needs of the local services but bearing in mind individual preferences. The transfer schemes included a residual clause to ensure that no one became unemployed by being left out of the rearrangement: the Memorandum issued in August 1973 prescribed a residual authority for each case where a former local authority area was to be divided, the residual authority to be responsible for any employee not moved elsewhere by the local transfer scheme. A similar problem arose where a function was divided. The former county boroughs had sole responsibility for highway maintenance within their boundaries: after reorganisation this duty was split between county and district. The operative principle here was that the new employer should be the authority responsible for the greater part of the employee's former duties. Wherever this was uncertain or open to dispute, a local transfer scheme had to be made. The same applied to staff engaged on functions that became concurrent between counties and districts under the 1972 Act, e.g. parks and open spaces. Anyone absent from normal duties due to secondment or training was to be treated as if they were at their normal place of work on the transfer date unless it had been a condition of the secondment or training that a move should be made subsequently to another employer. An agency agreement created a situation for which there could be no general rule: the local agreement had to decide whether staff were to be employed by the principal or the agent. A further problem arises here as to the effect on staff of any subsequent amendment or termination of an agency arrangement. Staff were protected from redundancy or hardship due to reorganisation through provision of compensation—should this protection be extended to cover changes in agency? The DOE answer was 'No' because alterations in agency should be regarded as an aspect of the continuous management process in local government and not as a delayed part of the 1974 reorganisation. But it was accepted that staff should have safeguards against this possible source of adversity. The DOE Memorandum *Transfer and Protection of Staff* indicated that such protection should be written into applications under Section 110 of the 1972 Act which authorised the Secretary of State to arbitrate wherever there was disagreement between local authorities over the nature or extent of agency agreements.

Local transfer schemes created opportunities for dispute both between local authorities and in relation to individual officers. Disputes between authorities were subject to arbitration by the Secretary of State. Individual cases were referred to hardship tribunals.[14] They were concerned either with the precise nature of an officer's duties prior to reorganisation or whether the terms of the transfer order had been applied correctly.

There remains the question of what principles should govern the protection of staff interests. Under Section 255 of the Local Government Act 1972 there were two parts of the process. The first stage lasted from 1 April 1974 until an officer was given a written statement of new terms and conditions of service: within this period, irrespective of the nature of his new duties, an officer was entitled to terms and conditions not less favourable than those previously enjoyed. After the written notice was served, i.e. stage two of the operation, the protection of terms of service continued but salary was adjusted to whatever level was appropriate for the duties now being performed. Where an officer was posted to a less responsible position, his salary fell but compensation was payable under Section 259 of the 1972 Act.

These general rules were subject to detailed modifications. Many officers had received extra payment for the additional work caused by the preparations for reorganisation. This supplementary pay was not covered by the protection arrangements. If any national pay award were agreed between 1 April 1974 and the date when an individual officer received his written statement, then for the purposes of comparability of salary and possible compensation his salary as at 31 March 1974 was regarded as having been increased by the amount of the salary award. Officers given appointments by the new authorities before 1 April 1974 had the same degree of protection as those transferred on that date. The Order[15] covering protection of staff interests also required local authorities to reimburse staff for additional travelling, removal and incidental expenses wherever these were caused by a move required by the reorganisation—whether the actual move took place before or after 1 April 1974. A wide discretionary power was made available to meet particular problems, e.g. variations in property values between different areas.

A major difficulty arose from the possibility that adjacent authorities being merged together might have given different gradings to similar jobs. Section 255 makes it quite clear that a salary could not be lowered where an officer continued to perform substantially the same duties. So the anomaly could not be ended by reducing an officer's grade. The Memorandum *Transfer and Protection of Staff* stressed that there could be no justification, either, for upgrading merely to avoid anomalies, particularly in view of the counter-inflation legislation. Both sides of the national negotiating bodies did agree that such upgrading should be eschewed. The effect was to continue unequal treatment of people doing similar work. Inevitably, not all staff were happy after reorganisation. Those who had not got the sort of post they hoped to achieve felt frustrated. For some, ambition exceeded ability. Others, perhaps, were unlucky. A job in a larger organisation can mean less scope and more monotony. To assist those who wished to move the Local Government Staff Commission established a jobs bureau, and authorities were asked to inform the Commission of posts due to be advertised nationally. The Commission also organised a mutual job-exchange service.

Beyond doubt, local government staff were well cared for in this process of reorganisation. NALGO had good reason to be satisfied with the treatment of its members. Indeed, as shown below,[16] there was some public feeling that officials had done rather too well out of the reshuffle.

An officer dissatisfied with his transfer to a new authority could appeal. Appeals machinery was established in January 1974 after consultation with the interested parties including NALGO. It had two stages. The first was a hearing within the local authority at which the grievance would be ventilated. The local authority for this purpose was the council by which the officer was currently employed—so these initial hearings were sometimes conducted by the 'old' authorities which had to notify the other 'new' authorities concerned. Some difficulties were ironed out satisfactorily at this stage. But where an officer was not content with the result of the local hearing he could carry his case to the second stage, a Staff Appeals Tribunal. These tribunals consisted of five members, two representing the employers' side of the provincial council, two representing the staff side of the provincial council and an independent chairman appointed by the Local Government Staff Commission. Most chairmen were recently retired senior local government officers. Where tribunals could not reach unanimous verdicts, decisions were based on a majority vote: thus the chairman exercised decisive influence. Provision was made for special advisers to assist tribunals on technical and specialised matters, but these advisers had no vote. In order to speed up the settlement of disputes, notice of appeal to a tribunal had to be given within two months of receipt of the decision from the local hearing unless the Staff Commission agreed that in a particular case the time limit should not be enforced.

On what grounds could an appeal be made against transfer or the conditions of transfer? These fell into three broad categories: the nature, terms or conditions of previous employment; the nature, terms and conditions of the new employment; or personal hardship arising from the transfer or proposed transfer. Thus there could be dispute over whether the general principles of a transfer order had been applied correctly or reasonably to a particular case in regard to an officer's former duties or to the location of his employment. There could be dispute about whether new duties were reasonably comparable with former duties. Under hardship the range of possible pleas was extensive. They included the difficulties, financial and personal, of moving home not merely for the officer himself but also for members of his family; increased expense and personal inconvenience of longer journeys to work; special problems of officers in poor health or otherwise disabled; the effect of transfer on opportunities for study leave or further professional education. The clause covering other members of the family had wide ramifications. It covered disturbance of wife's employment, disturbance of children's education or employment, and the extent of an officer's family responsibilities for persons needing care. Thus a spinster caring for an aged parent was within the scope of the hardship provision. It was also possible to appeal not against transfer but against failure to pay compensation for the disturbance or extra travelling cost caused by transfer or against failure to retain more favourable conditions of employment enjoyed before reorganisation. It was not intended that appeals should succeed where an officer complained of his ignorance of the new post or merely preferred to work for one authority or one service rather than another.

The preparations made to handle appeals were, in fact, unnecessarily elaborate because so few cases were pressed to the stage of going before a tribunal. In the district covering East Anglia and the south-east region north of the Thames a total of four appeals were heard. The low number is indicative of the negligible amount of redundancy and the generous policy of local authorities. Some of the appeals lodged were against the nature of the alternative employment offered; the hope was that the tribunal would find the offer unsuitable or unreasonable so that the appellant would become eligible for compensation.

Salary scales and establishments

Early in the discussions on reorganisation the local authorities accepted that the salary structure for chief officers would have to be renegotiated. The existing salary agreements for Clerks and chief officers were due to expire on 1 July 1973 so that, irrespective of reorganisation, fresh action was needed. An aggravating factor was that some authorities had been in the habit of making payments in excess of the agreed scale; this caused dissatisfaction and resentment among those who did not get favoured treatment and was irritating to central government which likes public servants to be remunerated on the basis of uniform scales. So a new formula was required that would be strictly applied. Apart from the cost of living there were other factors that helped to push up salary levels. It was claimed that the new breed of Chief Executives would have wider responsibilities for overall management than Clerks had had in the past. It was also argued that the new local authorities would have a wider range of functions and that this would be reflected in the pay of top officials. The latter argument proved to be largely mistaken since later legislation removed personal health services, water and sewerage to other bodies. However, the loss of these services was not known or at least accepted by local authorities when these pay negotiations started.

Salaries of local government officers are agreed through a complex system of joint committees representing employers and staff. The employer's side is represented through the associations of local authorities. The pattern of employee representation varies. Chief officers have their own associations to speak for them. At lower levels the employees are represented through one or more trade unions. Within this framework discussions on new salary scales for Chief Executives started in 1972. Then came Stage One of the Conservative Government's counter-inflation policy with its total freeze on pay increases and negotiations. So the discussions were suspended and were not resumed until early in 1973. Agreement on the salary scales for Chief Executives was not reached until March 1973. The policy of pay restraint then produced further delay as the agreement had then to be submitted to the Pay Board to see if it fell within the terms of the Pay Code. Not until 11 June 1973 were local authorities informed that the new scale was permissible. By now some Chief Executives in the counties had been selected. It followed that these posts had to be offered on the basis that the terms proposed were subject to sanction by the Pay Board. This introduced a temporary but unexpected element of uncertainty into making the appointments.

The salary scale for Chief Executives is related to the population of their authorities. The Registrar-General's estimate of static population is used for this purpose but it can be adjusted upwards for a variety of causes. Account can be taken of projected increases in population and of fluctuations caused by daily influxes of workers or seasonal migrations of holiday visitors. Fluctuations below 50,000 or 15 per cent of the static population are ignored and each 'fluctuating person' is counted as not more than one-fourth of a regular inhabitant. Previously some Clerks had received additional payments for extra duties. All such fees, other than those as returning officers payable under Sections 41 and 42 of the 1972 Act, are now incorporated in basic salaries. In exceptional circumstances further payment is permitted where a Chief Executive assumes a responsibility that extends beyond the area of his own authority, e.g. as Clerk of a combined police authority.

Agreement on Chief Executives' pay was followed by negotiations covering that of other chief officers. New salary scales were announced on 19 June. Again, this was after some appointments had been made. Again, the scales needed the sanction of the Pay Board. So the terms offered to the new chief officers were clouded by a penumbra of doubt over the possible reaction of the Pay Board. These salary scales are based on a complex formula which leaves an element of discretion to individual local authorities. There are two basic criteria: population and the scope and responsibility of a particular post. An element of flexibility is essential since local authorities still have wide variations in their departmental and management structures. Posts with the same title in authorities of similar size can still be of very different importance. So there are two stages in fixing the salary of a chief officer. The population group of his authority has to be determined by the same rules as those used for Chief Executives. A 'fulcrum point' salary is related to each population group and this becomes the centre point of a scale which extends normally to three increments above and three increments below the fulcrum. The individual officer is then allocated to a point on the scale depending upon the responsibilities of his post. To be two or three increments above the fulcrum a chief officer has to be a member of the management team, to be in charge of a group of departments or an exceptionally large single department which is involved substantially with all the activities of the local authority. A Treasurer would fit this specification. To be on the fulcrum point itself an officer has to be the head of a department responsible to the council through a committee but he would not be on the management team. The lower end of the scale, fulcrum minus two or three increments, applies to heads of minor departments who are subject to direction by another chief officer. A further upward adjustment can be made for special local factors, e.g. responsibilities arising from the management of a municipal airport. But in no case can salary exceed fulcrum plus four increments. Deputies receive up to 75 per cent of the salary of the chief officer of their department.

The reaction of the Pay Board to this settlement was ambiguous and became more so. Early in August local authorities were informed that the agreement did not appear to conflict with the requirements of the Pay Code. However, because of the element of discretion involved the Board wished to be told of individual salary proposals before they could be regarded as approved. Local councils started to send in details of proposed salaries with supporting justification to the Joint Negotiating Committee for transmission to the Pay Board. Meanwhile it was understood that the proposed salaries could not be paid nor firm contractual agreements be concluded with new chief officers. In mid-August, having studied returns from the local authorities, the Pay Board agreed that the proposed salaries could be accepted where the average salary level for chief officers did not exceed the fulcrum plus two increments. The Board stated that it would examine all cases where proposed salaries exceeded fulcrum plus two and it would also examine the pay proposals of a random sample of local authorities which came below this level.

At this stage the Pay Board came under pressure to take a firmer line with local authorities. There had been controversy in some areas over the proposed remuneration of senior officials, and the matter was complicated because the reaction of political parties was not uniform. Some Labour groups were happy to be generous, to be good employers and perhaps have some conflict with the Pay Board: other Labour groups felt that top salaries were unreasonably high and that the cause of social justice would be best served by a restrictive interpretation of national agreements. Some Conservatives wanted their council to have chief officers of the highest possible calibre and were prepared to pay to attract or retain the best talent available. Other Conservatives, conscious of the burden on ratepayers, preferred lower salaries. A few councils protested that their neighbours, by upgrading staff, engaged in unfair competition for staff: Bradford complained in this way about West Yorkshire. The question of grading was particularly sensitive in relation to middle-ranking professional staff. Another source of criticism found no public expression but was not unimportant. Senior civil servants noted that pay parities between local government and the civil service had changed to the disadvantage of the latter. The knowledge that the Chief Executive of a large county was to be paid more than a Deputy Secretary was ill-received in Whitehall. In particular it was felt that chief officers of the metropolitan counties were overpaid; these authorities have the highest populations and so pay the highest salaries, but their range of activities and expenditure is less than that of the shire counties. Quite apart from questions of pay, there was also concern over the numbers of staff the new authorities proposed to recruit, for their planned establishments were often greatly in excess of the combined staff of the authorities being replaced.

These grumblings did not achieve great national publicity. Nevertheless a feeling grew that the new councils were having insufficient regard for the needs of economy. Some councillors wrote to MPs. Some MPs got in touch with Ministers or with the Pay Board. Early in October the Pay Board stressed that amalgamation of authorities was not itself an adequate reason for upgrading posts. The Board reminded local authorities that it had power to require justification for grading. The implication was that if the Board could not approve gradings then an authority might receive an order to lower the salaries paid. Meanwhile thousands of middle rank appointments were being made, and it is difficult to see how the Pay Board could have kept an effective check on all that was being done. The strain under which the Pay Board operated no doubt explains the curious letter sent to the staff side of the Joint Negotiating Committee for Chief Officers late in November. The Pay Board complained in the letter that it had not received the information for which it had asked about proposed salaries for individual chief officers (such information had been supplied). It explained that the Board approved settlements and not enabling agreements. (In June the Board had seemed to approve the agreements concerning Chief Executives.[17]) The letter also said: 'The introduction of new salaries need not wait upon the prior approval of the Pay Board, though this must not be taken to imply that such approval will in due course be forthcoming.' Apparently this meant that salaries agreed locally could be paid but if the Board subsequently disapproved then there would have to be some downward adjustment. Such a move would have caused great ill-feeling; its effect on staff behaviour at a critical period is unpredictable.

Faced with this amber light the Joint Negotiating Committee offered to continue to advise local authorities about proposed salaries in order to minimise the risk that the sums paid would not pass the scrutiny of the Pay Board. The Joint Committee seemed to envisage that it might be called upon to defend individual local authorities against the Pay Board and did not wish to be faced with cases that departed widely from the accepted norms. Meanwhile the Pay Board indicated its intention of undertaking a fuller survey of staffing costs based on a sample of local authorities. The enquiry was to cover both the size of the paybill before and after reorganisation and changes in the number of employees. The Pay Board was subsequently dissuaded from this course of action because of the exceptional burden it would have placed on the authorities selected for examination.

Meanwhile the House of Commons reflected the considerable public feeling that senior local government officers were obtaining too much financial benefit from reorganisation. Mr Graham Page, the Minister of State for Local Government, commented in January 1974: 'Some of the opinions which have been expressed are exaggerated and some are ill-informed, but some cannot be disregarded.'[18] As a result of this criticism, and to avert further action by the Pay Board, the Local Authorities' Conditions of Service Advisory Board undertook a survey of comparative staff costs before and after reorganisation. The survey excluded London and was restricted to administrative, professional, technical and clerical staff because the pay of other main groups of local authority employees, i.e. teachers, police, firemen and manual workers, was not greatly affected by reorganisation.

There were very considerable difficulties in carrying out a survey in the winter months of 1974. Not only was this the peak period of preparation for the changeover on 1 April but office work had been disrupted by the fuel crisis and the attendant three-day working week. In this turmoil local authorities were asked to submit to LACSAB a statement of the number of staff employed and the paybill on 1 April 1973 together with a comparable estimate for 1 April 1974. Staff to be transferred to the new health and water authorities were excluded. Salaries paid in 1973 had to be grossed up by the amount of the increases payable from July in order to make the comparison more accurate. The survey was based on paybills rather than establishments because in April 1973 some posts had been left vacant in anticipation of reorganisation and because it was clear that not all the staff provided for in formal establishments could in fact be recruited by April 1974. Insofar as recruitment continued after April 1974, the survey underestimated increases in staffing costs—a factor which LACSAB omitted to emphasise. Another difficulty was that some authorities did not know until virtually the last minute how many staff they would have under the new regime because the allocation of functions controlled by agency agreements had not been settled. Inevitably there must have been some intelligent anticipation in the figures sent to LACSAB. Detailed scrutiny of the results shows that local authorities responded to the survey rather differently. In the circumstances this was to be expected.

Ultimately over 96 per cent of the new county and district councils supplied information and only sixteen authorities failed to reply. Among the sixteen were some of the larger authorities with the most acute internal difficulties. Before assessing the results it is essential to give a fairly detailed account of how the information gleaned from local councils was presented. First was given the number of posts and the total paybill in April 1973—subject to the adjustments mentioned above. Then came the parallel figures for April 1974 followed by a comparison showing the rise or fall in numbers and cost. Then a further series of figures showed the position 'after deducting explainable increases'. Local authorities had been asked to estimate the effect on staff numbers and salary cost of a variety of factors; these increases were then deducted from the 1974 figures and the result was compared with the 1973 return. When this curious exercise was completed most authorities could show a reduction in staff numbers and salary cost as compared with the previous year because the amounts covered by the explanation were greater than the actual increases. Where this was not the case the authority was in effect reporting inexplicable rises in staff and salaries.

An extensive catalogue of reasons for more staff was proffered. It covered additional statutory functions, agency work not previously undertaken, improved local standards of service, functions transferred from other local authorities, work undertaken previously by consultants, the expansion of existing services, upgrading of staff into categories covered by the survey, underestablishment and unfilled vacancies in April 1973, the rent rebate scheme, the implementation of the Bains Report, the need to man offices in areas split by reorganisation, enforced computerisation and staff retiring soon after April 1974.[19] In addition salary costs, but not the number of employees, were affected by increments due on 1 April 1974 and by the regulations covering salary preservation for officers moving to less responsible posts. Clearly some of these categories overlap but in total they provide a vast range of 'explanation'. It does seem remarkable that some councils did not account for their staff increases under one or other of these headings. Was this the result of a certain casualness or a measure of honesty in the way information was supplied?

The reasons given for increases in staff vary greatly in importance. To transfer responsibilities from one council to another should not, in general, cause a net addition to employment. The decision to give development control to the districts must be costly because counties scrutinise district actions to ensure that the interests of the county are secure; so there must be some duplication of planning staff. The Bains Report caused more attention to be paid to management and personnel work but the cost of additional appointments in this area should subsequently be offset by economies resulting from more efficient organisation. Movement of staff from the manual grades had been caused by reorganisation where amalgamating authorities had varied practices in the designation of supervisory staff: such a situation created pressure to equate gradings in the way most favourable to the employees concerned. So the figures for increased staff mask a very small saving in manual staff. They also make a saving in the use of outside assistance, e.g. architects in private practice.

The central results of this investigation were that salary costs had increased by 9·4 per cent, the number of staff by 4·7 per cent and average salaries by 4·5 per cent. But these national figures conceal considerable variations which are illustrated in the tables below. The first one gives a simple comparison of staff employed in 1973 and 1974. The second table compares staff figures for 1973 with those for 1974 after deduction of the 'explained increases'. At this stage the unsatisfactory nature of the survey becomes apparent. Some authorities which reported no overall additions to staff failed to analyse why some sectors of their staff had increased in spite of the fact that some of the reasons for making extra appointments must have affected them. And it will be seen that a few councils reported no change in the number employed. Thus the West Midlands reported a staff of 1,593 in April 1974 and a staff employed by their predecessors on comparable duties in April 1973 of 1,593. At this stage one may express disbelief combined with sympathy for busy people who have to fill up questionnaires.

COMPARISON OF STAFF EMPLOYED *April 1973–April 1974*

Change in staff	Metropolitan counties	Shire counties	Metropolitan districts
Decrease	3	15	8
No change	1	—	—
Increase up to 5%	—	7	11
Increase above 5%	1	15	16
No return	1	2	1

The authorities who failed to produce a return were Tyne and Wear, Avon and Knowsley, all of which faced exceptional starting troubles. Cleveland produced a joint return for the county and its districts which for the purposes of the table above is classified as no return. Easily the largest increase was reported by Leicestershire with a rise of 70·7 per cent.

COMPARISON OF STAFF EMPLOYED AFTER DEDUCTION OF 'EXPLAINED' INCREASES

Change	Metropolitan counties	Shire counties	Metropolitan districts
Decrease above 10%	2	16	15
Decrease up to 10%	3	5	9
No change	—	5[20]	5[21]
Increase	—	11[22]	6[23]
No return	1	2	1

Ten authorities reported no change in the second table, i.e. their explained increase was made to correspond with their actual increase. Seventeen councils reported an increase in staff which exceeded the additional numbers accounted for by the varied explanations: to suggest that these councils have been unduly wasteful, or more wasteful than other authorities, may not be justified. The difference may lie largely in the way they chose to complete the LACSAB questionnaire. Lancashire, Staffordshire and Bradford gave scale increments due on 1 April 1974 as the sole reason for additional cost. Nine councils[24] produced no explanation at all: since their staffs were equally eligible for scale increments it is apparent that the analysis supplied by these authorities was incomplete.

Another criticism facing local government was that it had permitted unreasonable pay increases for individual officials either through the new scales for chief officers or by the regrading of individual posts. These factors were in addition to the increases obtained by promotion to more responsible positions. According to the LACSAB survey the average salary of administrative, professional, technical and clerical staff increased from £1,914 in April 1973 to £2,001 in April 1974, an increase of 4·5 per cent. The 1973 figure was grossed up to include the pay award of July 1973 and the 1974 figure includes the normal annual increments payable in April. However, the variations from the average are rather greater than might be expected.

CHANGE IN AVERAGE SALARIES 1973–1974

Change	Metropolitan counties	Shire counties	Metropolitan districts
Increase above 5%	3	7	16
Increase up to 5%	2	25	13
No change	—	—	1
Decrease up to 2%	—	5	2
Decrease above 2%	—	—	3
No return	1	2	1

The single no change return came from the City of Manchester with an average salary of £1,810 in both 1973 and 1974. The largest increases were reported by North Tyneside (29·9 per cent), Greater Manchester (23·3 per cent) and Lancashire (14·8 per cent). The biggest fall was at Gateshead (4·1 per cent) and, among the shire counties, at Kent (1·7 per cent). It is notable that all metropolitan counties pay above average salaries and the highest average reported by any authority was £2,302 at South Yorkshire. The best pay of shire county staff was at Humberside (£2,251 average) and the best pay of metropolitan district staff was at Rotherham (£2,218 average).[25] Lowest averages were reported from Suffolk (£1,630) for the shire counties and from Solihull (£1,722) for metropolitan districts.

One would not wish to labour the inadequacies of the LACSAB survey. It was produced in haste under difficult conditions. Nevertheless, the material about explanation of rises in staff members is so curious and erratic as to be valueless. The report laid stress on the fall in chief officer posts and the total cost of their salaries, but this was an inevitable consequence of forming fewer local authorities, and was only marginally the result of local decisions. The real tests of what the new councils were doing was the total of staff employed and their average salary. The report accepted that salary scales below chief officer level had not been subjected to the same degree of national scrutiny as those for chief officers.

The overall growth in employment of 4·7 per cent[26] is unsurprising in view of the desire to get the new authorities off to a good start in terms of standards of service combined with the desire to avoid redundancy. Having recorded the 4·7 per cent increase the report went on to assert: 'but there are reasons why the number of staff could have increased by 9·3 per cent'. This statement was based on the calculation that after subtracting explainable increases the staff had declined over the year by 4·6 per cent. Similarly the 9·4 per cent growth in salary costs was accompanied by the comment that 'reasons can be advanced why costs should have risen by 12 per cent'. The rationale here was that after explainable increases had been subtracted from the 1974 paybill the result was 2·6 per cent below the 1973 paybill. The evidence on which these conclusions are based is far too unsatisfactory to support any precise figures. It has been shown that local authorities treated the survey in various ways. Some chose to provide no explanations: had they produced a full analysis the figures for explainable increases would have been higher. And granted the way the survey was organised almost anything could have been explained.

Had the local authorities been forced to incur extra expense on staffing against their wills, then one would expect the greatest increase in cost to arise where structural disturbance was greatest. But this was not the case. The five shires which had no boundary change reported an average increase in staffing cost of 10·6 per cent: the remaining shires reported an average increase of 8·3 per cent. Since the cost comparisons must have been easier in the shires that retained the same territory, it is likely that their figures are more accurate. The implication seems to be that cost increases were caused by the policies of individual councils rather than by the implacable requirements of structural change. Perhaps the fairest assessment is that the quality of the evidence assembled for the LACSAB survey is too poor for any firm conclusions to be drawn.

The response of the Pay Board to this unconvincing publication was an attempt to organise a more detailed enquiry into salary levels of three authorities: West Yorkshire, South Glamorgan and the Lancaster District. However, this enterprise was inconclusive, partly because the Board was dissolved before the investigation could be fully completed. The Board's recommendations were that local government salaries should be related to those of other public bodies and that there should be no extension of population-based salary agreements.

Early retirement and compensation provisions
It was widely accepted that the pattern of senior appointments made during the reorganisation of London government in 1964 was most unsatisfactory. The general policy had been no redundancy and no detriment. No one was to lose his job and no one was to be downgraded. So wherever two or more former authorities were joined together to form a new London borough, potentially there were two or more chief officers for each top post in the new structure. The position was eased by some retirements and some chief officers managed to move to posts outside London. But there was still much duplication at the top levels with Town Clerks working side by side with Associate Town Clerks, Treasurers working with Associate Treasurers and so on. The staffing establishment was top-heavy. The result was not only uneconomic but it led to confusion in lines of responsibility, duplication and jealousy. Many working arrangements were initially agreed on a temporary basis but once established became difficult to change.[27]

The Government resolved that this should not occur again in the wider reorganisation of local authorities. The Redcliffe-Maud Royal Commission had specifically recommended that a repetition of the London situation must be avoided,[28] possibly through changes in the regulations governing loss of office. It was clear that chief officers would be more affected than other staff because the reduction in the number of authorities must cut the total of such posts. Their societies represented to the Government that reorganisation would hit them more seriously than other grades of staff because of the loss of status and independence if a chief officer were forced to step down to a second-tier post. There was a precedent for more generous early retirement regulations as the Civil Service had made its own rules more flexible because the decline of the Empire had cut the number of posts abroad. So the solution was to encourage early retirement by chief officers and their deputies over the age of fifty: Section 260 of the 1972 Act authorised a scheme to achieve this objective.

Inevitably, the details were complex. The basic feature was that up to fifteen years might be added nominally to the service of a chief officer or a deputy for purposes of pension entitlement, provided that the number of years added did not exceed the number of years actually served. Thus it was possible for those with twenty-five years' service and who had reached the age of fifty on 1 April 1974 to retire on full pension. One limitation was that the pension received was not protected against changes in the cost of living until the age of fifty-five, so anyone who did retire in 1974 at the age of fifty was taking a gamble on the rate of inflation until 1979. But this risk was offset by the provision that entitlement to a pension would be unaffected by other employment unless the new job was covered by the same superannuation scheme. So a solicitor aged fifty with fifteen years' local authority service could go into private law practice and still receive the pension. This provision gave rise to a number of anomalies: a Chief Education Officer covered by the teachers' superannuation scheme could resign and take another post within local government and still obtain his pension. Another limitation was that the early retirement provisions applied only to those with a minimum of five years' service—but there must have been few chief officers and deputies who could not meet this requirement.

The scheme did raise awkward questions of definition. Who were chief officers? The nature of departmental organisation varies between local authorities and the concept of 'chief officer' was and is a matter of local interpretation. Ultimately it was agreed that the scheme should be extended to 'recognised officers' who were accepted locally as being responsible for the work of a department and who tendered technical advice to a committee. A further condition was that their salaries had to be at least two-thirds of those of the chief officers of the authority who were recognised as such by the national negotiating machinery for chief officers' salaries. As a result of this adjustment some Housing Managers and Chief Public Health Inspectors were brought within the arrangements. However, Divisional Education Officers were not included. These officials served divisional education committees within counties: where the division was coterminous with a single county district they had come to be treated as a chief officer of the district.[29] Yet they were formally on the staff of the county LEA and were no more than third-level officers within that organisation.

Officers covered by the early retirement scheme had to exercise their option by 28 February 1974. Their decision had to be given to their existing employer, which had a power of veto exercisable within a month. They had no right of appeal against a veto but there was an assumption that no such veto would be imposed. The final date for choice was extremely late in the timetable of reorganisation. No doubt, it was arranged to give maximum opportunity to those concerned to consider their employment and other prospects. The retirement regulations[30] were not formally published until July 1973, although their main outlines had been known in advance. This date was after many chief officer appointments to the new authorities had been made. A few of the newly chosen chief officers thereupon decided to retire, thus causing confusion and delay in making subordinate appointments while their own jobs were re-advertised at a stage when many of the best qualified candidates had found situations elsewhere.

The early retirement scheme was open to criticism as being unreasonably generous and expensive. Its effect was also uncertain since it was impossible to foretell how many of those eligible would take the chance to leave local government. Obviously it was hoped that the older and less vigorous would go because they would be less likely to obtain top positions in the new system. Equally, some of the more adventurous spirits just over fifty might decide to take a pension and start a fresh career. Many able chief officers did go and local authorities lost valuable experience. The final result was that the intention to avoid a surplus of chief officers was duly achieved. Some deputies became chief officers; new deputies were promoted from the ranks below; even a few third-level officers from large authorities became chief officers in smaller authorities. With many opportunities to move up the ladder, the average age of chief officers fell. But after 1974 the chances of promotion for senior staff will be poor: not only has reorganisation reduced the number of chief officer posts quite dramatically but the number of vacancies in the first years after 1974 will be below average. There is a prospect of frustration for able and ambitious men at present holding third- and fourth-level posts.

As the early retirement provisions had such an important effect on local authorities, it is worth stressing that they were the product of a ministerial decision and were not based on the collective wisdom of the associations of local authorities. They were, in fact, an aspect of central government determination to encourage a more modern Bains-style approach to local management through more energetic chief officials.

A separate set of regulations[31] covered compensation for redundancy and loss of salary due to reorganisation. There was no question here of exercising a choice. Nor was there a minimum age limit. A local government officer of any rank who failed to obtain a local government post with equivalent salary was compensated and this arrangement covered chief officers and deputies below the age of fifty.

There were three parts to the compensation system: single lump-sum payments to those with limited service, long-term compensation payable until retirement, and compensation on retirement. Lump-sum payments were for officers with a minimum of two years' service (which could include in aggregate breaks of up to six months' duration) who lost their jobs and had not been offered reasonably comparable employment by a public authority. But the payment was reduced to anyone within three years of retirement and it amounted to 13–30 weeks' pay reduced by any amounts receivable under the Redundancy Payments Act 1965. For officers with a minimum of five years' service, which might include breaks of up to a year at any one time, a regular payment was made equal to one-sixtieth of loss of income for each year of service. This scale was increased for people over the age of forty subject to a maximum of two-thirds of the lost pay. However, compensation was reduced when alternative employment was obtained or superannuation was payable. For compensation on retirement the qualification was the same as for long-term compensation. Local government pensions depend in part upon the length of service of the individual officer, so the pensions for people who had lost their jobs were augmented by crediting them with additional years of service. This benefit was restricted to officers made redundant at or above the age of forty: they were credited with additional service related to the extent of their service after reaching this age, subject to a maximum credit of fifteen years or the number that could be accrued before normal retirement—whichever was the less. Pensions can be reduced at the discretion of the compensating authority if other employment is obtained.

Necessarily, difficulties must develop in the administration of such a complex set of rules. As compensation depended on loss of pay, the level of an officer's pay was of critical importance. Should the calculations include or ignore a temporary increase in payment due to promotion to a higher acting rank? The ruling here depended on the circumstances under which the acting rank was attained.

Where the previous holder of a post left for reasons unconnected with the reorganisation, then the acting rank counted for compensation purposes; where the acting rank applied for a short period prior to 1 April 1974 and was conferred because a senior officer had moved to another post due to the reorganisation, then the acting rank was ignored. Long-term compensation was open to review in relation to pay received from other employment and hardship arising from the diminution of such alternative income.

A compensation scheme of this kind must create opportunities for dispute. Anyone aggrieved by a compensation award could appeal to an industrial tribunal. It also encouraged local authorities to reappoint chief officers and their deputies below the age of fifty because failure to do so could produce a substantial claim for recompense for loss of office. Indeed, only one case was reported of a chief officer below fifty failing to gain reappointment. The new Derbyshire County Council decided to appoint the deputy county surveyor of the former Derbyshire as Surveyor to the new authority. The former Surveyor, Mr Race, aged 49, was estimated to be entitled to about £100,000 as compensation for loss of office. Had Mr Race been a year older the matter could have been handled under the early retirement regulations.

NOTES

1. Joyce Long has shown from a study of staff reactions to earlier reorganisations between 1966 and 1968 in Teesside, Torbay and the West Midlands that staff of the larger authorities were more likely to feel satisfied by the effects of change than staff from the smaller authorities. See *Local Government Studies* (June 1973), No. 5, pp. 47–57.
2. For a full report on this research see the *Local Government Chronicle* for 9 and 23 November 1973, 22 February and 8 March 1974.
3. 1970–1, Cmnd 4584, para. 51.
4. NALGO Local Government Reorganisation Information Bulletin 2/71, pp. 8–9.
5. See p. 40.
6. London Government Staff Commission, see its Report issued by HMSO in 1966.
7. NALGO Reorganisation Information Bulletin 6/72, p. 4.
8. LGSC 1/72, paras 7 and 8, issued in July 1972.
9. In the case of Directors of Social Services, these authorities were required to consult with the DHSS. After such consultation the permission of the Staff Commission might be sought for a national advertisement excluding London. Under the Local Authority Social Services Act, 1970, the Secretary of State must approve the qualifications of Directors of Social Services. The appointments made by Birmingham and Sandwell were not accepted.
10. See pp. 149–52.
11. The order in which interviews were held and thus the order in which appointments were offered was important. In the summer of 1973 there were many

interviews for chief officer posts and a council that acted rapidly could expect a wider field of candidates. The Local Government Staff Commission offered to try and timetable interviews to minimise the possibility that candidates would be asked to go to different places on the same day. Some councils accepted this offer; others did not.

12. J. Long and A. Norton, *Setting up the New Authorities* (Knight, 1972), p. 70, stressed the importance of giving equal treatment to applicants irrespective of their previous employers.
13. The policy was given statutory force by Statutory Instrument 1847 of 1973 issued under Section 255 of the 1972 Act.
14. See pp. 137–9.
15. The Local Government (New Councils) Order, SI 444 of 1973.
16. See p. 143.
17. The actual words were 'the agreement seems to have been devised with proper regard for the requirements of the Pay Code'.
18. HC Deb., Vol. 867, col. 1696.
19. LACSAB, *Survey of Local Authorities' Salaries* (May 1974), Schedule C and Appendix A.
20. Cornwall, Devon, Essex, Kent and Surrey.
21. Manchester, Barnsley, Sheffield, Dudley and Sandwell.
22. Bedfordshire, Buckinghamshire, Derbyshire, Hampshire, Hertfordshire, Isle of Wight, Lincolnshire, Northamptonshire, Salop, Staffordshire and Wiltshire.
23. Trafford, Gateshead, South Tyneside, Birmingham, Coventry and Calderdale.
24. Cheshire, Cumbria, Humberside, North Yorkshire, West Sussex, South Yorkshire, Salford, Rotherham and Gateshead.
25. As property prices in the Sheffield and Humberside region are among the lowest in England, it does seem that local government officers in this area have a higher standard of living than their colleagues elsewhere.
26. The figures in this paragraph cover Wales as well as England outside London.
27. Enid Wistrich, *Local Government Reorganisation: The First Years of Camden* (London Borough of Camden, 1972), pp. 270–1.
28. Report, para. 564; 1968–9, Cmnd 4040, xxxviii.
29. Peter G. Richards, *Delegation in Local Government* (Allen & Unwin, 1956), p. 68.
30. SI 1260 of 1973.
31. SI 463 of 1974.

Chapter 7

FINANCE

The Weakness of the 1972 Act
The financial section of the Local Government Act 1972 is modest and uncontroversial. It is concerned largely with the expenses and receipts of local authorities and the audit of their accounts. The general provisions for financial administration represent the re-enactment of the parallel sections of the now repealed Local Government Act 1933, but slightly adjusted to meet new conditions. Many of the issues that faced finance departments through the disturbance of reorganisation were discussed above in Chapter 3. This chapter deals with the broad questions of the cost of reorganisation and the extent to which the 1972 Act made adequate preparations to enable local authorities to carry heavier financial burdens.

The sparsity of the financial part of the Act reflects the extent to which the economic consequences of reorganisation were overlooked in the many stages of the public debate that preceded the introduction of this measure. The financial memorandum which accompanied the publication of the Bill in 1971 stated that the Bill 'will have little direct effect upon either local authority finance or expenditure overall'. Indeed, the speech of the Secretary of State, Mr Peter Walker, in the second reading debate made no mention of the cost of the reform. The one aspect of local finance that had attracted widespread attention was the rating system; there was virtually unanimous agreement that it was both inadequate and unfair. But the Conservative Government omitted any changes in rating from the reorganisation Bill. A supplementary measure to provide the financial complement to the general reform was promised for the following session 1972–3. However there was further delay and the legislation did not appear until the autumn of 1973. It authorised some changes in central government grants and extended the rate rebate scheme, but only negligible alterations were proposed in the law of rating. This Bill reached the Statute Book in a last minute scramble before Parliament was dissolved for the general election of February 1974. Had the election been held two or three weeks earlier, which at one stage seemed probable, then the Bill would have fallen and could not have been enacted by 1 April 1974.

Thus the possible reform of local finance was treated apart from other aspects of reorganisation. There was no government initiative to make major policy innovations. Doubtless the topic was politically embarrassing. The 1971 Green Paper, *The Future Shape of Local Government Finance* (Cmnd 4741), had demonstrated a lack of determination to strengthen local taxation. The expense of the new system and how to meet it were questions not adequately faced. This expense was not simply a matter of paying the bills that arose from moving from one structure to another. The very fact of reform created an expectation that things would be different and better—better in the sense that improved services would be made available. A psychological and administrative climate was created favourable to change and extra cost. There is no sign that Ministers had thought of the financial consequences of the mood that their legislation was to create.

The 1972 Act repealed the requirement that local authorities must appoint a Treasurer: instead, Section 151 requires local authorities to 'make arrangements for the proper administration of their financial affairs and [to] secure that one of their officers has responsibility for the administration of these affairs'. Since local councils still appoint Treasurers who are the same sort of people with the same sort of qualifications, it is arguable that Section 151 makes no difference in practice. However, the responsibilities of a Treasurer are unique. In *Attorney General v. de Winton*[1] it was held that a Treasurer is not the mere servant of his council but had a direct financial relationship to the burgesses and could not plead the orders of his employing authority as justification for an unlawful act. Whether an officer appointed under Section 151 without the title of Treasurer is covered by the rule in *de Winton* is not known. Meanwhile the law has given new recognition to financial officers. They are now statutorily responsible for the form of the accounts kept, for the control and maintenance of accounts and for signing the local authority's balance sheet. Further, they are to have access to all records for the purpose of internal audit.[2]

Another requirement withdrawn by the 1972 Act was the instruction to county councils to appoint a Finance Committee. This requirement had always been an anomaly: why should counties have been subjected to this control which did not apply to other types of authority? One suspects that the provision was repealed not because it was anomalous but because it was incompatible with the modern emphasis on local determination of management structures, and because it might well impede moves towards corporate planning. But has the general move to replace Finance Committees by Policy and Resources Committees weakened cost consciousness? Finance Committees were advised by Treasurers. A Policy and Resources Committee looks to its Chief Executive, and sometimes, to other chief officers, as well as to its Treasurer. Dr Marshall has described the Finance Committee as 'a permanent watchdog'.[3] In many authorities the watchdog function has been split between the Policy and Resources Committee and its finance sub-committee. Has this damaged the quality of financial control? Other authorities, e.g. Leicestershire and the West Midlands, have retained a full committee, separate from their central policy committee, to scrutinise expenditure. The value of this arrangement would repay further study.

The Rating System

Two sections of the 1972 Act sought to minimise variations in the level of local rates. One is temporary; the other is voluntary, of limited geographical application and unused. These provisions are of much less importance than originally anticipated because the effect of differential rating designed to smooth over differences has been swamped by the great escalation of rate poundages.

The temporary scheme is designed to reduce changes in rate levels as between different parts of the same rating authority. Before 1974 there was a tradition that rates in rural areas were lower than those in urban areas because fewer services were provided. Now the urban/rural distinction has ended, rural areas will have to contribute towards the cost of all services, some of which may be too distant to be of great advantage to rural ratepayers. Villagers are now required to help to pay for the sports centre, the swimming pool and the museum in their market town. To soften the blow to the countryside of a large jump in their rates, a programme of differential rating was introduced to spread the increase over a maximum of five years.

In the shires the scheme operates at both county and district levels: in metropolitan areas it applies only at district level. The first step is to ascertain the rates required for county purposes in each county in 1973–4 and for equivalent purposes in the former county boroughs in the same period. In making precepts for county purposes any differences are abated at the rate of 2p a year or where the initial difference is greater than 10p by four equal reductions in successive years. Any initial variation of less than 2p is ignored.[4] So relief for an initial variation of 3p amounted to 1p in 1974–5 and ended thereafter. Similarly, the districts calculate the rate required for general district purposes in different parts of their area in 1973–4 and proceed to abate the variations in the way described above. Naturally this scheme applies only where county or district boundaries have changed. For example, in the Isle of Wight differential rating applies simply within districts. In former county boroughs or former districts that continue with unchanged boundaries as second-tier authorities, differential rating applies only to county functions.

An inevitable consequence of the 1972 Act is that the lower rates in rural areas will be ended rapidly. Indeed, the situation will be reversed, and rural rates will tend to be slightly higher. Where a third-tier parish or town council spends money it will impose an additional precept on local occupiers. Urban areas without third-tier local government will be spared this extra burden. The result may be to encourage town and parish councils to try and have local needs provided by county or district authorities and so avoid any added local charge.

As noted above the second type of differential rating authorised by the 1972 Act has not been used. Under Section 170 the districts within a metropolitan county may agree to reduce disparities in their rate poundages. Such a scheme has existed in London for over a century and was designed originally to spread more evenly the cost of poor relief between the richer and poorer parts of the capital. The cost of national assistance has long since passed to the Exchequer. However, it is arguable that the central core of each conurbation contains highly-rated shop and commercial premises which serve the whole of the contiguous built-up area and that the benefit of these high valuations should be shared by the whole metropolitan county. Yet since the resources element of the Rate Support Grant already gives extra financial help to authorities with lower rateable values per head, the case for further redistribution is weakened. So Section 170 remains unused.

The reduction in the number of local councils has cut the number of rating authorities in the English provinces from 1165 to 332. But in some districts the process of levying the rate became more complex. Rates in rural areas had always been more intricate because of the additional parish rates. The parishes continue to operate and in some places have been joined by new third-tier authorities formed from former urban authorities that have lost their second-tier status. Within one district these bodies exist side by side with areas without third-tier institutions. In addition, the introduction in 1966 of domestic relief to residential occupiers tripled the number of separate rate levels: each rating authority has to levy a rate for non-residential occupiers, a reduced rate for residential occupiers and an in-between rate allowing half the full domestic relief for mixed hereditaments. Another complication, described above, is the temporary differential rating.

The total effect is best illustrated by reference to a specific example. Leeds Metropolitan District includes the former County Borough of Leeds, two former non-county boroughs, five former urban districts and twenty-eight parishes drawn from three former rural districts. Parish precepts and differential rating mean that each of these thirty-six locations may have a separate rate poundage. As domestic relief requires three scales of charge in each area, Leeds can levy 108 distinct local rates.

Payment of Councillors
Section 173 of the Local Government Act 1972 provides for the payment of an attendance allowance, in effect a fee. to members of county and district councils engaged on approved duties connected with council business. A maximum rate of payment of £10 a day was fixed by the Government. Within this limit each local council can decide the conditions governing payment, e.g. the rate for part of a day and the definition of approved duties. Travelling and subsistence expenses are also refunded on a national scale.

The principle of payment is not wholly new. The Local Government Act 1948 had instituted a financial loss allowance for council members who could show they would lose income from their employment as a result of coming to council and committee meetings.[5] But the payment of attendance fees under Section 173 differs from the 1948 provision in two respects. All councillors are fully entitled to the attendance fee whether or not they are employed. Further, the attendance fee is taxable whereas the financial loss allowance was not. So while the £10 a day is much higher than the £5.50 financial loss allowance, the added benefit for a councillor who had received the allowance and now pays tax on his attendance fees is not very great. The advantage of the new system is greatest for councillors ineligible for the financial loss payments, in particular housewives and retired people. Inevitably the cost of remuneration of councillors has increased substantially. In addition, travelling and subsistence expenses are higher because larger authorities require councillors to travel greater distances and be away from home for longer periods.

In terms of the total budget of local authorities the sums involved are not large. But this expenditure is or can be a highly sensitive matter. The total bill for a county of average size can easily exceed £1,000 a week. If a figure of this kind is widely publicised the public may express resentment, especially at a time of agitation over increases in local rates. There may develop a feeling that councillors are lining their pockets at the ratepayers' expense. In fact, if a leading member of a large authority spends a full five-day week on council business he will earn £50, which is no more than the *average* salary of local government office workers if the latter's entitlement to paid holidays is taken into account. £10 a day is around a third or a quarter of the amount paid to chief officers who advise councillors. Quite obviously this sum is far below the scale of remuneration that councillors with professional or managerial occupations could expect to earn.

Nevertheless, the issue of payment is still delicate. It can scarcely become a point of dispute between the political parties since the attendance allowance was introduced by a Conservative Government and supported by the Opposition parties. Locally some Conservatives have favoured more restrictive rules governing payment, but the differences have not been serious.

Unfortunately it is true that the piecework method of payment could encourage some councillors to multiply or extend committee meetings. If payment encourages elected representatives to delve into detail then it will become inimical to modern concepts of efficient management. This tendency could be avoided if councillors were paid a fixed sum irrespective of the time taken by their public duties. The problem would be to decide the amount of the fixed sum. Were it too low, then leading members of councils would receive inadequate recompense for their services. Were it too high, then the less active backbench councillors would be overpaid. If an additional fee were available for council and committee chairmen, then a fresh and unfortunate element of patronage would enter into the election of chairmen.

Nostalgia for the ideal of an unpaid public service still exists. How far the payments affect the behaviour of local councillors is likely to depend upon how much publicity they attract. If local papers continue to print detailed reports of how much money each individual councillor has received from public funds, it is possible that public sensitivity will remain high. This could have a variety of effects. More councillors may feel encouraged to claim less than their full entitlement. Some may claim nothing at all. There could be pressure to reduce committee meetings because of their cost. There may be greater hesitation about sending councillors on long

journeys at council expense. It is not impossible that publication of
the sums received by councillors could influence elections. A sitting
councillor who was known to have received £1,000 a year or more
as a result of his public responsibilities could be at a disadvantage
against a challenger without council experience. This handicap
could be most severe for an influential member of a major authority
who had devoted most time to council affairs and who had received
the most money. There could be an advantage at election times for
wealthy councillors who can afford to minimise their claims. If the
attendance fees become a constant source of public comment it is
probable that some councillors will drop out of local government
while other people will be deterred from standing for election
because of the sneer that those who seek office do so for financial
gain.

Alternatively the topic may fade away. Local newspapers may
stop publishing information about payments. Local political groups
may agree, explicitly or otherwise, not to raise the matter. The
public may come to accept that democratic representation cannot be
organised without expense.

Reasons for Rate Increases
Without doubt the major public concern over local government in
1974 was not with reorganisation as such but with the substantial
rise in local rates. The increase was commonly above 50 per cent.
At Barnsley it was 100 per cent. The rates have long been an
unpopular tax. They are criticised for being unfair and their inci-
dence has no relation to ability to pay. Rates are extremely visible.
The ratepayer is very conscious of what he has to pay. The greater
part of income tax is deducted when income is paid to the recipient:
indirect tax is lost in the cost of goods and services obtained. None
of these palliatives eases the collection of rates. So the unpre-
cedented increases in 1974 brought a storm of protest and an uprush
of ratepayers' associations. At Solihull the District Council, under
pressure from local ratepayers, tried to start a campaign to end two-
tier government in metropolitan areas. Solihull, with the lowest staff
cost of any metropolitan district, claimed that the two-tier system
was wasteful and that it had caused a dramatic rise in cost without
corresponding benefit. Of course, this was a cry for the return of lost
county borough status and resentment by a Conservative district at
being engulfed in a Labour-dominated county. But the local rate
rise of 92 per cent was a fair reason for strong feelings. Solihull was
atypical in urging further changes in local government structure but
its reaction to the rates situation reflected a national mood. A

F

Commons debate about rating on 27 June 1974 led to a defeat for the minority Labour Government in spite of a promise to establish a committee of enquiry into local government finance. With a further general election expected shortly, the Government announced in July 1974 an extra measure of relief to domestic ratepayers whose bills had gone up by more than 20 per cent.

The reasons for rate increases can be divided into three broad categories. Some have nothing to do with reorganisation; some are indirectly associated with it; some are a direct consequence of the 1972 Act.

Two important factors were quite unconnected with reorganisation. Inflation was responsible for cost increases of the order of 15–20 per cent. The distribution of the rate support grant was determined by government policy under separate legislation. The Conservative Government has decided to change the balance between the three elements in the grant and to allocate the domestic relief element on the basis of a complex formula instead of at a uniform level. The newly elected Labour Government rapidly decided to revert to a flat rate within an unchanged total grant except that aid for Welsh authorities would be much greater. Thus domestic relief was fixed at 13p in England and 33.5p in Wales.

It was possible, of course, to work out whether a particular authority would have been better off under the Conservative distribution or the Labour distribution. Alternatively the domestic relief for 1973–4 could be compared with that for 1974–5. But none of the major decisions affecting the rate support grant had any necessary connection with reorganisation. They did, however, affect local administration by adding to the difficulties of the newly formed finance departments of rating authorities. Rate demands were delayed. In some areas the demand notices, normally issued in March, were not distributed till May or June. Possibly this postponement softened the shock of the higher rates and prevented even fiercer public reaction. It is also arguable that postponement weakened the link in the public mind between reorganisation and higher rates. Neither of these propositions is capable of proof.

The Water Act 1973, which transferred water and sewerage functions to regional water authorities, is a contemporary aspect of the reform of local government but was not an inevitable consequence of it. However, the Water Act had a major impact on local rates. The new water authorities were empowered to impose a sewage charge and a water charge to be collected with the local rates. These charges were substantially higher than the previous sewage and water rates and led to complaints from councillors and the public.

The new water authorities faced heavy expense in creating a new organisation, but they also made provision to build up reserve funds and to protect themselves against inflation. It was argued that the scale of these contingency provisions was unreasonably large. It was also argued that their capital development schemes were not subjected to the same degree of critical scrutiny as those of local authorities. The district councils cannot effectively challenge these levies; they can but collect the money and pass it on. A majority of the members of the water boards are nominated by local authorities but there is no direct accountability to the public. Indeed, very few people will know who are these nominees. It may be that these bodies are effectively dominated by professional opinion and that the financial consequences of their activities is given insufficient consideration. Without doubt, the water authorities aggravated the rate increases.

Another effect of reorganisation was to encourage councils to run down cash balances. Normally they keep some money in hand to cope with unforeseen events. The balances may accumulate because some expenditure included in estimates is not incurred. Alternatively, the forecasting of rate revenue may be a little pessimistic. But by March 1973 these 'kitties' had largely disappeared. Inflation was one cause. Another was that many councils decided to reduce their balances so that the rate for 1973-4 could be kept as low as possible. Sometimes this was done for political reasons, as the rate for 1973-4 was fixed just before the elections for the new shadow authorities. Where an authority was being divided or amalgamated there was also reluctance to pass on liquid assets to the new councils.[6] Thus the 1973-4 rate tended to be below what was needed to meet current expenditure. This under-rating, combined with the disappearance of balances, explains a part of the jump in the 1974-5 rate poundages.

The third group of reasons for rate increases stems directly from the reorganisation. There are obvious causes of greater expenditure in relation to accommodation, staffing, equipment and policy developments for particular services. The varying degree of difficulty involved in establishing the new authorities was described in Chapter 3. The LACSAB survey on increased staff costs was discussed in a section of the previous chapter. It was shown that the survey failed to analyse clearly how additional expense had been incurred—how far was it due to additional appointments, higher salary scales, regrading and payments arising from early retirement or the compensation provisions? In the turmoil of reorganisation the costing exercise needed to answer these questions would have been difficult, if not impossible, to complete.

The shadow authorities started off with a proper determination to make the new system work well. The initial concern was to create a viable and progressive organisation. In this atmosphere cost consciousness tended to slip into second place. Newly appointed chief officers recommended generous establishments for their departments. Their proposals were influenced by the ideal of a high quality of service combined with a desire to protect the interests of local staff. No doubt they were aware that it would be easier to obtain resources at the inaugural stage rather than in later years when the new structure had developed greater rigidity. The much higher penny rate products of the new authorities may have induced councillors to be unusually open-handed. Certainly they seem to have been less vigilant than is normal. It is understandable that they wished to avoid deflating the enthusiasm of newly appointed chief officers by severe pruning of their initial proposals. Sometimes reality broke in when it became clear that people were not available to match the proposed establishment. Total costs of the new organisations emerged after establishments had been agreed. Normal checks on over-generous staffing were missing. Detailed scrutiny by management services units was impossible since these did not exist in the early weeks of a shadow authority unless it was virtually a continuation of an outgoing council. Comparison with the past was also impossible because a new situation had developed.

Additional staff was not the only cause of extra costs. The new councils wished to improve standards. Much of the extra expenditure was beyond their control in that they had to complete projects already started by the outgoing councils. Where authorities were merged or responsibilities had been handed on to the upper tier, there had been a tendency in 1972 and 1973 to start schemes in the knowledge that the cost would be shared ultimately over a wider area. Another significant cause of added expenditure was that many new authorities inherited different policies from their predecessors relating to the same function. Many examples are given in Chapter 5. These variations had to be ironed out especially where monetary charges or benefits to individuals were involved. Inevitably there was pressure to accept the more generous policies.

The initial budgets of the shadow authorities simply could not be prepared with the precision and attention to past practice that is usual in local government. Comparison with the previous year's figures is a stern discipline. The new Finance Departments gathered together material on the spending of their predecessors but the exercise was full of difficulty. In any case changes in area and changes in function undermine the force of past experience. When guidelines are weakened the whole situation becomes more fluid. There is less to check the voices that urge more of this or more of that.[7]

Elected councillors bear constitutional responsibility for local authority expenditure but they can fairly plead in great measure to have been faced with circumstances beyond their control. Inflation led to price increases and national wage settlements they had to accept. In 1973 they entered on new duties with the optimism associated with the start of new ventures. Councillors dealt with problems as they were brought forward by officials and the total effects of their decisions on the rates was slow to emerge. The total cost was unknown until full information was available from the dying authorities about the cost of continuing their activities. This was particularly difficult to assess where authorities were being divided. The impact on rates was submerged by continuing uncertainty over the future of the rate support grant. In the autumn of 1973 few councillors were considering the possibility of rate increases between 50 per cent and 100 per cent in the coming year.

Ministers seemed equally ill-informed. A White Paper, *The Rate Support Grant 1974–5 (Cmnd 5532)*, published on 22 January, announced the financial assistance that local authorities could expect from central funds. It also stated that domestic rates should not rise by more than 9 per cent save in exceptional circumstances. Whether this forecast was based on inadequate information or was dictated by the prospect of a forthcoming election is not known.

Local government had been heavily involved in Ministers' attempts to cut expenditure. DOE Circular 77/73, issued in June 1973, indicated that for the purposes of the rate support grant the Government expected that local government expenditure would stay at the level then envisaged. This would involve reductions on some items, in particular cuts in highway maintenance. The Circular warned the shadow authorities: 'they should not assume it will be possible to provide in the first year all the administrative services they might wish'. How far this admonition had any effect is dubious. Cuts in capital programmes were made in October. Then in December DOE Circular 157/73 explained that the Government expected 20 per cent cuts in capital expenditure other than housing and 10 per cent cuts in the procurement of goods and services. However, pay and loan charges were unaffected. Another Circular, DOE 19/74, issued jointly by the departments concerned with local government, appeared after the 1974 White Paper on the rate support grant. It envisaged further cuts in a wide range of local services excluding housing and admitted that the standard of services might deteriorate. These policy statements emerged as part of a national economic strategy rather than as a result of concern about rates. They were also out of key with the relative optimism felt by the shadow authorities at the start of their existence.

Official estimates for the cost of the reorganisation were £23 million in 1973–4 and a further £15 million in 1974–5. These figures were produced by a joint working party of DOE and senior local government officers for the purposes of the rate support grant. They took account of factors which were likely to increase or reduce spending, e.g. computerisation, office accommodation, administrative savings (but not operational costs) due to the loss of health and sewerage functions, members' allowances, salary patterns for chief officers and early retirement. It must have been most difficult to arrive at any precise figures in view of the lack of firm information when these estimates were made. In any case they fail to reflect the cost of reorganisation for two main reasons. To subtract administrative savings from the loss of health and sewerage functions is to mask part of the bill. Even more important is the fact that the true cost of the 1972 Act must include the financial outcome of a myriad of optional local decisions which were not an inevitable consequence of reorganisation but which were encouraged by the general upheaval.

NOTES

1. (1906) 2 Ch. 106.
2. SI 1169 of 1974, paras 3–6.
3. On the function of finance committees see Dr A. H. Marshall, *Financial Management in Local Government* (Allen & Unwin, 1974), pp. 239–59. This work was, of course, written in the context of pre-1974 experience.
4. The Local Government (Differential Precepting and Rating) Order, SI 177 of 1974 authorised by Section 254 (f) of the 1972 Act.
5. This arrangement still applies to co-opted members of local authority committees.
6. Lancashire did have a substantial balance in hand on 31 March 1974 of which a due proportion was handed on to Greater Manchester and Merseyside. However, the distribution of this residue came too late to affect the rate demands for 1974–5. Elsewhere informal agreements were made about target figures for cash-in-hand on changeover day.
7. The Society of County Treasurers has performed a valuable service in producing annual analyses of county council expenditure. From 1974 onwards a new series of annual returns will appear that is based on estimates. These figures show comparative rates of expenditure per head on particular services as between different authorities. But the 1974 figures are of no help in assessing the overall cost of reorganisation.

Chapter 8

THE ASSOCIATIONS OF
LOCAL AUTHORITIES

The attempt at unification
The reorganisation of local government necessarily had a traumatic
effect on the associations of local authorities. Some were reconsti-
tuted; others disappeared. Before 1974 each type of authority had
its separate association save that the county boroughs and the non-
county boroughs worked together through the Association of
Municipal Corporations (AMC). The other organisations were the
County Councils Association (CCA), the Urban District Councils
Association (UDCA), the Rural District Councils Association
(RDCA) and the National Association of Parish Councils (NAPC).
In addition, there were two bodies concerned solely with education,
the Association of Education Committees (AEC) and the National
Association of Divisional Executives in Education (NADEE). At a
minimum the Local Government Act 1972 required the termination
of three of these institutions because the distinction between urban
and rural districts ended and the Act made no provision for the
delegation of educational administration to divisional executives.
But the impact of reform was so great that the whole pattern of the
associations had to be redesigned.

Basically the associations have three objectives. Like other pressure groups they are concerned to promote the interests of their
members and to provide a forum for discussion and a source of
advice for local authorities. These objectives have required a
measure of co-operation between the associations, particularly in
relation to negotiations with government departments and trade
unions, and also in connection with the establishment of a number
of joint agencies which have served all types of local authorities.
These joint endeavours included LACSAB, the Local Authorities
Conditions of Service Advisory Board; LAMIT, the Local Authorities Mutual Investment Trust; LAMSAC, the Local Authorities
Management Services Advisory Committee; LGIO, the Local
Government Information Office; LGTB, the Local Government
Training Board.

The volume of activity increased substantially in the post-war period due to two related factors. One was the need to resist the influence of central government and the other was the need to make local administration more efficient. The associations have managed to establish the principle that they should be drawn into preliminary consultations before government departments decide to undertake changes in local government law or practice: any failure to consult is now an automatic cause for complaint. Quite apart from the all-embracing issues surrounding the 1972 Act, the pace and complexity of change, or proposed change, in all the matters affecting local administration creates a fearsome burden of work. The associations monitor Bills that come before Parliament to see if their interests are affected; if so, it may be necessary to try and persuade friendly MPs or peers to put an association's view to Parliament. Vice-Presidents are chosen by the associations with this purpose in mind. There are constant consultations with government departments over the content of forthcoming Bills, Statutory Instruments and Circulars. Evidence is presented to official committees of enquiry. Matters raised by local authorities are pursued; these may involve important points of principle. Liaison is maintained with a large number of central representative bodies whose activities have some relation to local government. There is also an amount of international liaison with the EEC, the European Conference of Local Authorities and the International Union of Local Authorities.[1]

Without doubt the most important facet of all is the task of negotiation with central government. For this reason it was widely argued that the reorganisation of local government provided an opportunity to bring together the associations into a single organisation so that local government could speak to central government with one voice. Unity is strength. Various proposals had already been made which sought to strengthen and co-ordinate the work of the associations. In 1967 the Report of the Mallaby Committee, *Staffing of Local Government*, had urged the associations to establish a Central Staffing Organisation to survey staffing requirements and training needs and to publicise career opportunities in local government. At the same time the Maud Committee Report, *Management of Local Government,* advocated the establishment of a Local Government Central Office which would not only undertake the functions of the proposed Staffing Organisation but would also develop research and information services for local authorities and review the operation of all aspects of central control. Quite clearly, had the scheme of the Royal Commission been implemented for a structure of local administration based on unitary authorities, there would have emerged, if not a single association of local authorities, at least an association which occupied a dominant position. By 1972 the staffs of the existing associations were broadly in favour of the creation of a single, central institution. They felt that it would enable them to provide a better service for member authorities and so offer a better safeguard for the status of local government. A single association would produce a more attractive career structure and facilitate recruitment of high quality staff. It could also afford to develop research and statistical services and so provide fuller briefings for those sent to negotiate with ministers and civil servants. In the past the associations operated on a shoestring basis: their lack of resources was partially masked as local authorities allowed their chief officers to give expert advice to the associations without extra payment as part of their normal job. Obviously, a single institution could make far more adequate preparation for negotiations with central departments. It might also be in a sufficiently strong position to take initiatives instead of merely reacting to external pressures.

In October 1972 a meeting was held to consider the establishment of a Local Government Federation. The meeting was attended by representatives of the CCA, the AMC, the UDCA, the RDCA, the Greater London Council (GLC) and the London Boroughs Association (LBA). In broad outline the idea was to form a central Federation to which other associations would belong—each association representing a type or types of local authority. Each local authority would be eligible to join the appropriate association. The Federation was to be a strong body. It would employ all staff and provide the necessary services for the member associations. Committees of the Federation would review general policy, including local government finance. They would develop research and statistical services. They would assume responsibility for the existing joint acitivities, e.g. LGTB, LAMSAC, LACSAB. Other committees would specialise in particular functions of local government, e.g. education, social services, etc. Thus the AEC would be absorbed. There were also proposals for provincial sections of the Federation which, no doubt, would be particularly welcome in Wales. But the difficult question was how the policy of the proposed Federation was to be decided. The draft constitution had no firm recommendation on this crucial issue but it did include safeguards for the expression of minority views. A representative group within the council of the Federation or any of its committees could have its dissenting view recorded and, where appropriate, represented to outside bodies. This opened the prospect that the Federation would quite often be speaking with more than one voice.

Here was a bold plan to provide strong central representation for local authorities. Inevitably, it ran into difficulties. Over the years the existing associations had been in frequent conflict in the process of safeguarding the separate interests of their respective types of authorities. The new local government structure also contains different types of councils, and many leading figures in the associations found it difficult to envisage how future conflicts of interest could be effectively handled by a single federal body. Could the proposed Federation be a powerful influential institution if sometimes it had to speak with two (or more) voices? Another problem in 1972 was that nobody was in a legal or moral position to make firm decisions about the future of the local authority associations. These decisions had to be made by representatives nominated by the new authorities which were to be elected in 1973. No doubt had there been a substantial consensus of view about the way forward, detailed plans could have been made which probably would have been accepted by the nominees of the new authorities, particularly since there was considerable continuity of membership between the new authorities and the old. But such a consensus failed to develop.

When the details of the 'October constitution' were considered by the associations, they got a mixed reception. The CCA and the UDCA were broadly in favour. The RDCA and the LBA were more doubtful. But the fatal blow came from the AMC. In the early discussions the AMC, under the leadership of Alderman Sir Frank Marshall, had been strongly in favour of a unified approach to central government. The new Chairman of the AMC, Alderman Sir Robert Thomas, was far more critical and doubted the extent to which local government could speak with a single voice. The reason for this change of heart was political. Labour had made considerable gains at the borough elections of 1971 and 1972. Ultimately this produced a Labour majority in the AMC which feared it would be outvoted in a Federation representing all local authorities. Sir Robert Thomas was, in effect, expressing the determination of his Labour colleagues to have a separate organisation for urban areas which they were confident would be controlled by Labour supporters and used to oppose policies of the Conservative Government —especially in relation to housing.

The result was that a further meeting in April 1973 between representatives of the associations could agree only on a more modest objective. A statement urged the need for a central federation of local authority associations but was silent about the details of its constitution or functions. The new associations representing the new authorities were urged to consult together as rapidly as possible to create a new Federation and to ensure that there should be no redundancy among the staffs of the existing associations. Further, the new authorities were urged not to agree to the creation of a single organisation for any particular function until decisions had been made about a new Federation.

At this stage a fresh question arose. How would the new authorities line up when forming new associations? Would each type of authority have a separate association? Or would there be some merging? The surprise was the rapid and successful emergence of the idea for an Association of Metropolitan Authorities (AMA) which brought together all the conurbations. The AMA includes the metropolitan counties, the metropolitan districts, the Greater London Council and the London Boroughs. Two aspects of this Association are novel. The GLC and its predecessor the LCC had never previously joined an association of local authorities. The second feature was that for the first time upper and lower tier councils for the same areas were within the same association: the old AMC had included upper-tier county boroughs and lower-tier non-county boroughs but these were geographically separate. The constitution of the AMA permits each group within the membership to speak for itself when it feels it has a special interest to defend. If disputes arise between metropolitan counties and districts the AMA may possibly act as a conciliator but it will be in a weak and awkward position if it has to present conflicting views to outside bodies.[2] Indeed the arguments against the establishment of a central Federation of local authority associations would seem to be equally applicable to the AMA. But many of the leading critics of the Federation concept helped to form the AMA. Again, the reason for the apparent contradiction is political. In 1973 a large majority of the councils to come within the AMA ambit were Labour controlled. This immediate party identity overcame the prospect of future conflicts of interest between metropolitan counties and districts.[3] Also in 1973 the new metropolitan counties had not effectively established themselves. They had not developed policies; they commanded no loyalties. Metropolitan councillors tended to think of themselves as district representatives on a slightly remote and perhaps alien organisation.

London, of course, was an exception. The GLC was firmly established and was acutely aware of the possibility of conflict with second-tier authorities. Previously it had studiously stood apart from local authority associations; this exclusiveness helped to emphasise its unique size and status. So the decision to join with other provincial metropolitan areas was a distinct change of policy. Once again the basic reason was political. At national level the Labour Party took the view that as it controlled all metropolitan areas it was desirable that the Labour leadership in London should work with their provincial colleagues through a single association. No doubt the GLC was also confident that it could obtain separate access to the ear of Whitehall whenever the need arose.

The formation of a new Association of County Councils (ACC) was delayed by a further attempt to create a single insitution that could embrace all local authorities. A preliminary meeting held in May 1973 to establish the ACC voted unanimously that further discussions be held to try and form a singe body. It is notable that Labour supporters at this meeting were strongly in favour of a single body, no doubt because they felt they would always be out-voted in a separate ACC. This does demonstrate that the argument over a strong federal body was not a straightforward party issue. The further negotiations were fruitless because of the firm deter-mination of the metropolitan areas to have a separate organisation. So in July agreement was reached to form the ACC. Membership of the ACC was, of course, similar to that of the CCA. However, all counties, non-metropolitan and metropolitan, are eligible for mem-bership of the ACC. It is arguable that the six metropolitan counties and the GLC could obtain stronger representation of their interests working with other counties rather than with their own second-tier districts. Two metropolitan counties, South and West Yorkshire, did attend the preliminary meeting to form the ACC, and South Yorkshire was represented on the steering committee which drafted the constitution of the new body. Subsequently both these auth-orities joined the AMA and not the ACC.

A third major local authority association was formed by the non-metropolitan districts. This was a little more difficult to organise because the liaison required was more complex. The AMC acted as midwife for the AMA; the CCA did likewise for the ACC. But to bring the districts together required co-operation from the UDCA, the RDCA and the AMC. Difficulties in framing a constitution for the Association of District Councils (ADC) were also greater because of the variations in size of the authorities. The larger dis-tricts, the ex-county boroughs, headed by Bristol, felt that they should have permanent representation on the Association's govern-ing body—a claim which initially the smaller authorities were not prepared to concede. Utlimately it was agreed that districts with a population exceeding 200,000 should be entitled to permanent membership of the executive council. In fact, the largest districts had been unhappy about joing the ADC on any terms. The dozen largest districts made a joint approach to the ACC to gain admission to that body. Their case was that they had more in common with large authorities than small ones. Yet the driving motive was status-seeking. Big ex-county boroughs found it difficult to accept demotion to second rank authorities: acceptance within the ACC would have maintained their links with top-tier authorities. The ACC did not respond to these overtures for a variety of reasons. It did not wish to weaken the ADC or sour relations between the two associations. Had the dozen largest districts been admitted, there arose the obvious question: why not the thirteenth largest, the fourteenth largest and so on? Also the accession of districts would have greatly complicated the organisation of the ACC through the need to provide machinery to cover district interests, e.g. in relation to planning and housing.

The new local authority associations are significantly different from their forebears. There were changes in staff. Due perhaps to the uncertainty caused by reconstituting the associations, a high proportion of their senior staff moved on to other jobs. At a critical stage in the changeover half the establishment of senior posts in the ACC and the AMA were vacant. Even more important in creating a fresh atmosphere was the influx of representatives from local councils who had not previously served on national bodies. The new faces were younger and had stronger party affiliations—especially those from the shire counties. Before reorganisation the crucial difference between the CCA and the AMC was generally held to be that the AMC represented the urban industrial areas while the CCA stood for the green acres of the countryside. Such a picture was always an oversimplification since the AMC included many small country towns and the CCA covered some industrial and mining areas. Now the distinction is even less justified with substantial towns like Bristol, Nottingham, Leicester and Stoke contained within the ADC. In future the main divide between the associations is likely to be political. The AMA is Labour controlled. The majority of representatives on the central institutions of the ACC and ADC are Conservative in sympathy. Of course, this pattern may change with the ebb and flow of political fortunes. Stress on the party element also increases the significance of how local councils choose representatives on national bodies, particularly since in the ACC and the AMA each member council is entitled to send a delegation of three or more. The general tendency seems to be to send a team which represents the local political balance rather in the way that aldermanic seats used to be shared out between the parties. The alternative is for the local majority group, where there is one, to nominate the whole delegation. Again, the party battle increases the importance of how votes are held within the associations. In the defunct CCA, voting was by authorities: in the ACC each representative has a personal vote, so the voice from any one council could be divided. With the AMA such division is impossible since voting is by authorities. The ACC also permits the publication of the views of a minority category of member authorities where this differs from that of the ACC as a whole. In practice, this means that Welsh counties can and do issue separate opinions as the Welsh counties are predominantly Labour in political sympathies.

The creation of separate associations to represent the different types of local authority necessarily ended hopes of a strong federal body to represent local government at national level. Nevertheless, the element of co-operation between the associations has been further strengthened. All the joint activities sponsored by the former associations continue, with the sole exception of the Local Government Information Office. This came to an end because the AMA withdrew support as it wished to have its own press and information office: the ACC and the ADC felt unable to continue the LGIO without unanimous support from the associations. Full co-operation continued between the associations in relation to their international activities. A new field of joint activity developed with the establishment of the Central Council of Local Education Authorities (CCLEA) to act as a link between the education committees of the ACC and the AMA. The CCLEA also has a subordinate organisation, the Local Authorities Higher Education Committee (LAHEC) with its own specialist staff.[4] There is a strong case for extending this form of joint action to other local functions, particularly the police and fire services. Since planning is shared between counties and districts, and as planning problems overlap metropolitan and non-metropolitan boundaries, there is, in theory, a strong case for some national machinery through which local authorities can discuss these matters of common concern. Yet the issues here are so delicate that early action is unlikely.

So while there is no unified organisation to represent local government, the liaison between the associations is both considerable and increasing. It is idle to deny that there are substantial conflicts of attitude and interest. Equally, there is a considerable amount of goodwill. In particular, there is an informal agreement between the associations to try and find a building that will accommodate them all together with their satellite bodies. Should this prove possible, it would help the associations to work together even more closely.

Education—a special case?

The representation of local education authorities at national level raises issues connected with, but also distinct from, the reshaping of local authority associations. The basic contention was over whether education should continue to enjoy a separate, and some would say a privileged, position as compared with other local services.

Historically, the separate treatment of education goes back to the very inception of state schools in 1870. Local school boards, elected on a special franchise to protect minority religious interests, provided schools which offered elementary education. School boards could impose a rate precept on local rating authorities which the latter were required to pay. Necessarily this arrangement led to complaints about financial irresponsibility of the boards. They were abolished by the Education Act 1902 and multi-purpose local councils became responsible for state education which was extended to include more advanced courses than had been provided previously. Under the 1902 Act the local Education Committees enjoyed special status. They were entitled to have a proportion of co-opted members, being persons with special knowledge of education—this covered representatives of the churches and subsequently of teachers. Also Education Committees were required to meet in public. Even so, educational interests resented their assimilation into multi-purpose authorities and an Association of Education Committees was formed to stress their separate identity and to give state education an independent representative organ. No other local government function has had a powerful national body of this kind. The AEC aroused an amount of jealousy because education continued to be the most expensive local service and, indeed, has consumed an increasing percentage of the gross national product. Inasmuch as local services are in competition with each other for resources, education has been too successful to be popular with its competitors.

The disturbance caused by reorganisation created an opportunity to draw the AEC into a more broadly based institution or, alternatively, to bring it to an end. The position of the AEC had been weakened both by the Local Government Act 1958 and by the Bains Report. The 1958 Act removed the specific Exchequer grant for education and so made more direct the competition between local authority departments for financial resources. Even more important was the Bains philosophy of corporate management which insisted that local government activities should be viewed as a whole; education, therefore, should not be treated as a large and quasi-autonomous empire within local government. On this view the AEC became an anachronism.

As noted above, the early discussions on the reform of local authority associations envisaged a single national body, perhaps with a federal structure, to give local government a strong united voice. The AEC could have been brought into this model as the education committee of the comprehensive organisation. The AEC was ready to accept this arrangement subject to the right, when necessary, to express publicly its own opinions. At this stage of the negotiations it was agreed between the AMC, the CCA and the AEC that special arrangements for education must remain in the new system. The exact nature of this agreement has subsequently been a matter of dispute. The AEC case is that the other associations accepted that the AEC should continue: the alternative interpretation is that the agreement was that *the work* of the AEC should continue.

By the autumn of 1973 the idea of a single national organisation had become unacceptable. The ACC and AMA had been formed with a mutual desire to co-operate where possible. Education was an obvious avenue for co-operation. Both the ACC and AMA formed education committees[5] and the idea emerged for a bridge to be formed between these committees to be entitled the Local Government Central Council for Education. This plan entirely ignored the AEC. The AEC proposed a modified constitution for the LGCCE which gave it a tripartite basis founded upon the AEC and the education committees of the ACC and the AMA: the AEC would provide premises and a secretariat for the LGCCE. This scheme was extremely clumsy and involved duplicate representation. It was rejected by both the ACC and the AMA.

As the AMA and the ACC are vigorous bodies that represent all local authorities in England and Wales that have educational responsibilities, one might have expected that their attitude would have produced the immediate demise of the AEC. However, the AEC is continuing. There is still a feeling in some local Education Committees that they should continue to have a separate national voice. The AEC has a powerful Secretary, Sir William (now Lord) Alexander, who has held the post for many years and is reputed to be influential at the Department of Education and Science. The AEC also has a strong financial position so that it can continue for some time even if it suffers a drop in subscription income. This happy situation is the result of wise investment, successful publishing activities and economical administration through a small staff. One view is that the AEC is an example of a pressure group struggling to retain a position of privilege. The AEC argument is that its rival organisation will not be able to safeguard the interests of education. The bridge organisation—now styled the Central Council of Local Education Authorities (CCLEA)—deals only with matters on which there is agreement between the AMA and the ACC. Since these associations represent different types of area and are likely to have opposing political loyalties, they may often fail to agree on educational issues. Then any representations to the Government or other bodies connected with education are made separately by the AMA and the ACC. The AEC case is that if Ministers get conflicting advice from local government, they will ignore all advice and do as they, or their civil service advisers, see fit. Up to now the AEC has managed to avoid party controversy and has represented a consensus view to the DES. Its policy has been based largely on claims for more resources for education combined with emphasis on the need for maximum decentralisation of decisions on how these resources should be used. Since Education Committees include representatives of the teachers and churches, the AEC can also claim to represent a wider span of interests than the associations of local authorities; yet this claim is itself controversial since the role of teachers and churches on Education Committees is arguably undemocratic. The constitution of Education Committees has no parallel elsewhere in English local government.[6] Indeed, the interim report of the Bains Committee proposed that the statutory requirement to appoint Education Committees be ended so that local councils should have complete freedom to design their committee structure. Under strong pressure from the AEC, and no doubt elsewhere, the Conservative Government failed to respond to this recommendation. Yet this incident does show that the special position of education within local government does not pass unchallenged. Equally it is possible that if the AEC withers and the practice of corporate management is felt to frustrate educational aspirations, then demands may arise that education should be removed from local government. Such a move could reduce the burden of local rates. But the political objections would surely be overwhelming.

At the time of writing considerably less than half the local education authorities in England and Wales support the AEC. It has members among all types of education authority, English shires, Welsh counties, metropolitan districts and outer London boroughs. Politically the membership spans both Labour and Conservative

G

councils. Some councils rejected the wish of their Education Committees to be allowed to join. Elsewhere the decision not to join was taken initially by the Policy and Resources Committee and the view of the Education Committee was not sought. The strength of the CCLEA is that it embraces all local education authorities and not merely a cross-section of them. And the quality of its support is impressive since many local education chairmen serve on the education committees of the AMA and the ACC. In addition, the CCLEA has an important subordinate organisation, the Local Authorities Higher Education Committee: the latter has its own specialist staff and is likely to become a body of increasing importance.

It is essential for the AEC that it continues to receive recognition from the DES and other educational bodies—in 1973 the AEC appointed representatives to 125 national organisations concerned with education. In May 1974 the DES announced that the AEC would be removed from the Burnham Committees that negotiate salaries of teachers and other education staff. In future the DES will consult the AEC only on topics of general educational concern which are not exclusively matters for local education authorities. This restriction of recognition has weakened the AEC. Another source of weakness is the extent to which its influence has been built up around its longtime Secretary, Lord Alexander. Normally it is a mistake to stress the importance of an individual in a conflict of this nature. Nevertheless, Alexander is already beyond normal retirement age and his retirement has been postponed owing to the difficulties of obtaining a younger man of sufficient reputation to succeed him in the present uncertainty about the future of the AEC. Another unknown factor, which links back to the continued recognition of the AEC, is how far its rival, the CCLEA, can establish itself as an effective negotiating body. If its joint masters, the AMA and the ACC, commonly fail to agree, the AEC could still survive; otherwise, survival seems doubtful. This dilemma reflects the whole theme of the chapter. If the new associations of local authorities fail to reach common policies, their collective influence will fade and local government will be the poorer.

Professional Associations
A subsidiary effect of reorganisation was to stimulate a change in the pattern of associations formed by members of the various professions serving local government. These bodies are of two kinds. The mass membership organisations are concerned with professional qualifications and training. Other bodies have a limited

elite membership restricted to officers at or above a certain rank. A full study of these organisations would be a substantial work in itself. Only the most important developments are noted below.

Chief Executives have formed their own society. The code-name is SOLACE, the Society of Local Authority Chief Executives. Supported by a high subscription, SOLACE has a full-time Secretary and has adopted a range of objectives which include research. Previously the Clerks of the various types of councils organised themselves in separate associations. The important feature of SOLACE is that it embraces all principal authorities—counties and districts, metropolitan and non-metropolitan. Its constitution provides that members serving a particular type of authority may meet together as a separate section of the Society, but any section must consult the executive before publishing views on matters which affect Chief Executives as a whole. So although the varied types of local authority have failed to create a single national association, their Chief Executives have done so. However, SOLACE made a slightly unhappy start. It gave advice direct to a government department on a particularly delicate matter. This produced an immediate reaction in local government circles that the duty of SOLACE was to advise the local authority associations—and not Whitehall—in matters of relations between central and local government.

SOLACE decided to restrict membership strictly to Chief Executives, and to exclude deputies. This decision avoided awkward questions of who should be recognised as deputies. But it has also encouraged sectionalism at the second stage of the hierarchy. An Association of County Secretaries has been formed *inter alia* to support the claim that County Secretaries should be treated as chief officers in their own right. The long-established Society of County Treasurers is continuing. On the other hand, the County Architects Society and the City and Borough Architects Society have been brought together into a single body, the Society of Chief Architects of Local Authorities.

The changes in the field of finance involve much wider issues than those of status. The Institute of Municipal Treasurers and Accountants, which has been responsible for professional examinations, is now replaced by the Chartered Institute of Public Finance and Accountancy (CIPFA). The fresh title stresses that the new Institute is seeking to play a wider role in the area of public finance. It is co-operating with the Society of County Treasurers in attempting to improve the quality of financial statistics relating to local government. The title of its journal was also changed—from *Local Government Finance* to *Public Finance and Accountancy*. The alteration reflected the fact that some of the Institute's members had left local government to work with the new health and water authorities. It is arguable that the new title symbolises not only the wider responsibilities of financial officers but also the decline of local government.

NOTES

1. A survey of activities in the preceding year presented to the final annual conference of the Association of Municipal Corporations held at Bournemouth in September 1973 forms a deeply impressive record of the endeavours of one of the major local authority associations.

2. It has been the policy of the Labour Party that in metropolitan areas the responsibility for education should rest with the counties, not the districts. The return of a Labour Government in 1974 raised the possibility that this issue would be reopened. Such a move would be strenuously resisted by metropolitan districts irrespective of political complexion. On a matter of this kind the AMA would be hopelessly split and could exercise no influence.

3. Liverpool protested bitterly at its exclusion from the steering committee which drew up the constitution of the AMA. As one of the largest metropolitan districts Liverpool felt it had a right to representation: the council of the AMC had always included representatives from the six largest boroughs. The exclusion was political: the 1973 election failed to produce a political majority on the Liverpool Council but the Liberals were the largest party.

4. National representation of local education authorities is fully discussed in the following section.

5. The AMC and CCA had had education committees but they tended to play second fiddle to the AEC.

6. The Committee on Conduct in Local Government produced strong reasons why the co-option of teachers should be ended. But a majority of the Committee felt that the practice should be allowed to continue (1974, Cmnd 5636, paras 124–6).

Chapter 9

CONCLUSION

This chapter will not attempt to make any comprehensive assessment of the value of the Local Government Act 1972. To repeat what was said in the Preface, this book is offered as a study of the problems of moving from one administrative structure to another. It is not an attempt to assess the qualities and deficiencies of the new system. It is too early for this to be done. Indeed, perhaps a fair and full assessment can never be made. Local government is so fully integrated in the social and economic life of the community that it cannot be unaffected by any of the major domestic pressures. So the structural changes in local government cannot be separated from political changes, management reforms, the lack of national growth, inflation and the over-riding tendency for the Government to become more and more involved with all social problems.

Nor did the Local Government Act 1972 make such difference to how policy is formed by a local authority. Initiatives come from legislation, from government department Circulars, from local pressure groups and individual councillors or officers. Some policies are a by-product of other major decisions (e.g. to build a new town) or are accepted in a competitive spirit to keep abreast of other authorities. Occasionally major expenditure is forced by a major disaster. Nothing of this has been changed by altering the structure. Fewer and larger units of organisation make it more difficult for individual councillors to exercise great influence except by working through a political majority. Fewer units are likely to involve more uniformity in standards and so perhaps provide less opportunity for competitive situations to arise. But these basic relationships between local government and central government, between local government and the political parties remain unaltered. If the Act encouraged more party activity, facilitated central influence, strengthened the position of local government staffs and undermined the rating system by increasing expenditure, then it did no more than accelerate tendencies that existed already. The historian of the future is likely to regard the 1974 reorganisation as a stage in a continuing process rather than the start of a new era for local government.

Yet to regard reorganisation as an inexorable process lacking all surprise would be quite wrong. The important changes in management methods were not initiated by legislation: it will be argued below that the implications of these changes have not been fully examined. The financial outcome of reorganisation was an unpleasant surprise. To a lesser extent the effect of reorganisation on some local services was unintended. These themes will now be explored in reverse order.

What exactly were the intentions behind local government reform? The Royal Commission clearly hoped that a reformed system would have its scope extended to include functions now in the hands of nominated bodies.[1] The Maud Committee on Management urged that a general competence clause be added to the powers of local authorities.[2] All this presents a picture of wider horizons and opportunities for fresh initiatives. But the objectives set out in the Conservative White Paper on local government reform had a rather different flavour. There was emphasis on the need for decisions to be taken locally and on the need for economical administration of services.[3] No mention was made of expanding the scale of local government activities. Such expansion is contrary to Conservative political philosophy. Especially was this true of the early months of the Heath administration: the theme of the Conservative White Paper *The Reorganisation of Central Government* was that public administration had been 'attempting to do too much'.[4] So the concept behind the 1972 Act was that local government should be modernised, streamlined and made more efficient in terms of existing functions rather than it should be offered new fields to conquer. The failure of the subsequent Green Paper[5] to propose any major measures to improve the financial position of local authorities further strengthens this impression.

This difference in emphasis between the Royal Commission and the policy of the Conservative administration was largely unnoticed. Some councillors and many chief officers approached the task of building the new authorities in the expansionist spirit of the Royal Commission. So any suggestion that the Act had unintended results raises the question: unintended by whom? The fact that the desire of the Government to curb the growth of public services was not universally shared in local government circles explains why the outcome of the legislation was not always what its authors had hoped to achieve. Conservative opinion had not anticipated the growth in local staffing and the higher salaries. Whether the growth of services, particularly leisure and amenity facilities, went beyond the intentions of the Conservative White Paper is a matter for argument. As noted already these developments were encouraged because a small authority being absorbed in a larger unit could seize the chance of having a pleasant facility, e.g. a new or refurbished swimming pool, paid for by a wider group of ratepayers. In addition, some of the larger non-metropolitan district councils, particularly the former county boroughs, with substantial administrative resources needed an outlet for their energies. With education, social services and libraries all gone, their budget was a fraction of its former size. The temptation to spend a little more on leisure and recreational services was strong. The effect on the total rate bill would be trivial and it would help to provide justification for the prestigious and expensive central organisation of the district. In contrast, the shires and the metropolitan districts, saddled with the expensive personal services, were under severe financial pressures and had fewer spare resources for optional activities.

Chapter 7 has examined the reasons which forced large increases in rate poundages. The plight of local government finances in 1974 illustrates a fundamental problem of modern society. In the welfare state there are endless claims upon the public purse. One of the burdens of government, central and local, is to rank these claims in order of priority and to assess the total of expenditure that is tolerable. Because of the need for a national economic strategy and because of the high level of aid that local councils obtain from the national Exchequer, local financial decisions are subject to strong central influence. Nevertheless, the disturbance of reorganisation weakened temporarily the impact of national persuasion. The creation of new democratic institutions creates extra claims for public expenditure. The new institutions convey a sense of urgency so their claims cannot always be judged dispassionately against existing priorities. They insist they must get off to a good start. They can argue that they must be necessary, indeed vital, otherwise Parliament would not have created them. So the new organisations cost money. New faces, particularly in a first rush of enthusiasm, may be less unwilling to spend money. And the feeling grows that if rate demands become too severe then, in the end, the Government will be forced by political pressure to provide more grant aid. So the financial independence and responsibility of local authorities is further undermined.

Both the main political parties were surprised at the cost of reorganisation. Since neither party could evade some responsibility, the state of local government failed to become a major topic in the two general elections of 1974. It was convenient to avoid the issue. The idea that the new structure would be more efficient became unmentionable on a public platform. Expectations of new management techniques were battered somewhat unfairly since the new methods were not in full working order at the time when the shadow authorities had to take vital decisions.

One wonders how far councillors understand the nature of corporate management. Basically it involves an insistence that the problems and priorities of an organisation should be viewed as a whole. In terms of local government it requires that some councillors, the Policy and Resources Committee, shall have an overview of the affairs of the authority and that chief officers from all departments, supported by their chief assistants, shall work together in preparing advice for the elected representatives. The view that corporate management is inimical to democratic control is quite misplaced. Whether corporate management increases the influence of officials and reduces that of councillors—or *vice versa*—depends on how the system works in a particular place. Where councillors are effectively organised, corporate management should further strengthen their control over policy by providing a rational base for decisions. Naturally, this will not be the case where councillors are of poor quality and fail to co-operate among themselves. Personalities are also important, especially the personality of the Chief Executive.

Corporate management is an ideal at which to aim. The Bains proposals were just one means of achieving this objective. They proved to be very acceptable. Their adoption was due partly to pressure of time and work and partly to widespread support in political and official circles promoted by diverse and sometimes conflicting motives.[6] The Bains Report presented a straightforward account of contemporary management wisdom and applied it to local government. The political implications of the proposals were not covered. The Committee was prepared to produce supplementary material extending into this area but one of the local authority associations became reluctant to continue its financial support for the Committee. So it was wound up and a whole host of questions about how corporate management would work in local government were not asked. Inevitably the questions emerge as theory is put into practice.

How exactly is a management team supposed to work? What is to be the relationship between a Chief Executive and the other members? Is the Chief Executive to be thought of as an American-style presidential figure empowered, in the last resort, to over-rule all his advisers? Or should the Chief Executive act more in the manner of a British Prime Minister who is supposed to sum up the spirit of a Cabinet discussion while, no doubt, injecting an element of personal preference into the decisions finally recorded? And what is the strength of a decision by a management team? Are team members expected to show collective responsibility? If the management team makes a decision about education, must the Director of Education take the result to the Education Committee and defend it? How are the interests of a department not represented on the management team to be protected? If a chief officer is summoned to attend only when his department is under discussion, will he be at a disadvantage? If a chief officer presents proposals or information to the management team, will his committee chairman know what is being done before, after or never? One hears that a certain management team prepared an outline scheme showing the implications of X per cent increase in expenditure and further contingency plans showing the implications of (X–N) per cent growth should X per cent be politically unacceptable. If the local Policy and Resources Committee decided to accept the X per cent target would it ever know about the lower-level contingency scheme? Of course, the system of corporate management is not being applied properly if officials withhold material about alternative courses of action. Equally, it was possible for officials to suppress information in the days before the idea of corporate management had emerged. But greater co-operation among officials does increase the need for an adequate flow of information to councillors. Does local government need fresh safeguards to ensure that this flow is forthcoming?

The questions in the above paragraph are rarely asked in public. They raise issues that are often not settled by formal rules because of the difficulty of deciding what the rules should be. They will cause tensions and divided loyalties. When the tensions become too strong some aspect of a local controversy will burst through to the public ear.

Over the past months I have talked to a variety of chief officers about the operation of corporate management. I can report only that I have no clear idea of how it works. No doubt this is partly because there are variations in practice. A management team may operate almost as a secret society. Alternatively, it may generate sub-committees or working parties that are expected to report to the main body. The parallel is between the traditional pre-1914 Cabinet and the open-door Lloyd George-style War Cabinet. The latter is the more stimulating arrangement. A deputy chief officer asked to chair an inter-departmental working group and to present its report to the management team will be keen to make a good impression on his assembled senior colleagues. The membership of the management team is usually published but there are sometimes local conventions that permit chief officers to attend even when they are not members. Practice differs about whether deputies can attend. My impression is that members generally remain for the whole of a meeting but I have been told that some members remain only when they are interested in the agenda items. To get a balanced picture of the diversity one would have to be a fly on the wall at a number of management team meetings. Only in this way could a fair assessment be made of the atmosphere and the type of business conducted.

Chief Executives have told me that corporate management is working well; that it is not working well; that it will probably work well in the end when other chief officers come to understand and accept the system. This variety of response may reflect differing levels of local achievement or differing standards and expectations. It may be that some optimistic responses are caused by a feeling that academic enquiries should be met with a public relations front.

Resentment among councillors over corporate management is likely to be stronger if a council is not organised on firm party lines. Where an authority is run by a disciplined majority party, the local political leaders will feel themselves more securely in command of local officials. The Chief Executive will have an understanding, perhaps an unspoken understanding, with the most influential council members as to how affairs should be conducted. But where the activities of councillors are less co-ordinated, the functional committees and their chairmen will seek more freedom of action and be more suspicious of the influence of chief officers when they meet together. The management team may be seen as an interference with the prerogative of elected councillors to decide policy. One has heard of a chief officer who found it difficult to attend meetings of the management team owing to the hostility of his committee chairman. 'What's the point of wasting time going to the management team?' is a challenge that can be met either by discreet silence or by the prospect of a full-scale argument about the philosophy and practice of the corporate approach to local authority business. Mr Maurice Gaffney, the Somerset Chief Executive who lost his job after a few months in office, has said that his dismissal was due to dislike by influential councillors of his attempts to introduce corporate management. At Wirral the Education Committee insisted that it should report direct to the Council on matters of fundamental educational policy without the intervention of the Policy and Resources Committee or the management team; its recommendations could then be referred to the latter bodies for consideration of their financial implications. The argument was that only in this way could the Council be made fully aware of educational issues. This incident illustrates the danger that corporate management could restrict council debates to the allocation of resources immediately available to the authority. It is much easier to cut back programmes to make policies fit resources than to review resources imaginatively and so improve the extent to which they satisfy objectives.

Councillors have failed to provide a critical political dimension to their decisions on management structures. Leaders of highly drilled political groups felt that Bains-style proposals would help them to make crucial decisions in a more rational fashion. Conservatives were attracted by the idea of introducing business methods into local administration. Academic commentators generally avoided raising awkward issues. This requires some explanation. The fact is that members of university staffs interested in local government have tended to be more concerned with the theory of management and administration rather than with political science. Many have been recruited to provide training courses for local government staff. There was perhaps a natural feeling that it was important to encourage local authorities to take positive action on the broad lines of the Bains recommendations rather than to stimulate doubts about how some of the ideas might work in practice. And the study of management tends to concentrate on behavioural analysis of officials rather than elected representatives. So perhaps it was assumed too easily that councillors on new and larger authorities would and should readily adapt themselves to Bains-style institutions.

Yet a balanced picture of reorganisation must stress that it enabled great strides to be made towards treating the business of a local authority as a whole. The central policy committee, the Chief Executive and the management team have come to stay. How they mesh together will vary from place to place and from time to time.

The actual process of tranfer from the old regime to the new proved unremarkable. All important services continued without interruption. The press reported a little municipal junketing to commemorate the new system or to commiserate over the passing of the old. But no major items appeared on the theme of local administrative chaos. Indeed, the whole enterprise was an extremely smooth piece of social engineering. Of course there were delays in making fresh decisions. The outgoing authorities avoided issues during their last months of existence. The disturbance caused by the movement of staff meant that less urgent matters were set aside. Two months before the changeover, the Winchester Rural District Council, hard hit by staff transfers and illness of senior officers, appealed to councillors not to raise new problems. A few days before 1 April some buses owned by Hull Corporation were seized by a court official because the authority had failed to settle a debt of £48,000: the money was then paid and the problems of reorganisation were blamed for the oversight. Such incidents were exceptional. Some authorities with the greatest problems, e.g. the new shires, received much useful help from their neighbours. Particularly in view of the widespread criticism aroused by reorganisation, it is fair to record that senior administrative staff deserve much credit for the organisation of a relatively painless transition.

Whether reorganisation was so arranged as to help the making of wise decisions is a quite separate question. There can be no doubt that two factors greatly aggravated the task of preparation for the new system—the speed of the operation and the scale of the changes made. Should the changes have been slower and simpler?

It was stressed in Chapter 2 that the joint committees had no power to take action that would be binding on the new councils. Joint committees made detailed recommendations that were often highly influential in shaping future events; had the shadow authorities been given rather more time to study these ideas the final outcome might have been a little different. The lack of time became especially serious on matters where negotiations with outside parties were involved. The allocation and acquisition of office space would have been eased by giving wider powers to the joint committees or, alternatively, if the shadow authorities had been permitted a more generous timetable. Given a little more chance to think, the new councils might also have applied a more severe scrutiny to the proposed staff establishments.

The tyranny of the calendar gave added weight to the advice from central government. For hard pressed local staff this guidance became essential: it was received with gratitude similar to that shown by most of the Boards of Guardians after 1834 when they received advice from Chadwick on how to establish workhouses. However, the programme of central assistance and direction also fell behind schedule. Some of the issues, especially about property and pensions, were most intricate, and the preliminary discussions with interested parties took longer than expected. On agency the final ministerial directives had to wait upon the completion of local negotiations that took much longer than expected. Another cause of delay was the general election. For most of February and the first few days of March 1974 it was impossible to lay Statutory Instruments before Parliament because it had been dissolved. When the new Parliament assembled there was a rush of Instruments. Between 6 March and the end of the month, 39 Instruments were issued affecting local government, almost all being concerned with reorganisation. Fortunately they dealt with details and were uncontroversial. The new Secretary of State had virtually no time to change what had been decided before his arrival and any major parliamentary row over this delegated legislation could have caused severe administrative problems. The discipline of the timetable was hard on both central departments and local authorities. But in the end all went well.[7]

Was the time scale set for reorganisation too severe? Should there have been an extra three or six months' overlap between the old and the new? It is always easy to find reasons for delay. Nevertheless, the case for speed was overwhelming. The last few months of the old authorities became a twilight period when non-urgent business was pushed aside and decisions were evaded. Some councillors who were not elected to the new authorities began to lose interest. The interim period was also unsettling for officers concerned about their future employment prospects: a slower transition would have produced a longer period of uncertainty. A stiff schedule is a stimulating challenge which encourages effort. On balance my estimation is that the pace set for reorganisation was correct.

An allied theme is whether the scale of reorganisation was unnecessarily broad. Besides the changes of area and distribution of functions caused by the 1972 Act, water, sewerage and personal health services were transferred to other authorities. The abolition of aldermen reduced the experience of the new councils. In addition, the Bains Report encouraged major innovations in methods of conducting business. Would it have been wiser to postpone part of these reforms? Or are there advantages in the simultaneous shock treatment?

Granted that the decision had been made to take some services away from local government, it was certainly right to do this at the same time as the major reform. Otherwise adjustments would have been made to these services in 1974 to be followed by a further upheaval a little later on. Such a programme would have been absurd. Equally the optimum occasion for innovations in management was the moment when the new councils came to decide how to organise themselves. Had the Bains Report appeared some years later it would have been less effective because by then the new councils would have established practices which they were unwilling to change. The major obstacle to adopting fresh methods is always that old methods have their defenders because people are used to them. In a brand new organisation there are no traditions to defend. The abolition of aldermen also fitted the determination to get the councillors to think on radical lines. Quite apart from the objection that this form of representation is undemocratic, the absence of aldermen reduced the continuity between old authorities and the new and so aided the acceptance of change.

The inference is clear. If it is desired to make a number of structural changes in local government, then it is best to conflate them into a single, bold operation rather than subject local authorities to a series of lesser disturbances. It is unfortunate that some minor consequences of the 1972 Act have still to be tidied up. The pattern of the new electoral districts is not satisfactory because there was no time to sort out all local anomalies. So some new councils will soon suffer alterations in warding arrangements; the result will be more public confusion and more disturbance in the relationship between councillors and their constituents.

It is not argued that local government should be occasionally immersed in paroxysms of change with long periods of calm in between convulsions. While all aspects of structural reform should be brought together, other forms of change should be avoided at a time of general reorganisation. In this way the work flow for councillors and senior officials can be made more even. 1974 was not a good time to introduce fresh requirements in relation to existing services. The request from the DOE for the preparation of transport policies and plans might well have been postponed.

Another issue to be faced in any reorganisation is whether action is needed to stop 'dirty tricks'. Some outgoing councils took steps to influence the allocation of resources after their own demise. This applied particularly to authorities due to lose their identity in an amalgamation or, in the case of county boroughs, were to be demoted to second-tier status. The designation of the use of property was altered; schemes involving substantial capital expenditure were started; standards of service were improved; staff were upgraded. Many such decisions, no doubt, were fully justified, overdue and would have been made irrespective of the advent of the 1972 Act. Other cases invite scepticism. Fresh designations of property use made after 8 November 1973 were declared to be of no effect. The question is whether there should have been more similar controls. One solution would be to prohibit the dying authorities from making certain types of decision during their last year of life. But were this to be announced in advance, the deadline could be anticipated. Nor would a year be long enough, for many critical decisions were made in framing the budget for the final year. It is impossible to impose a long moratorium on local government prior to reorganisation. The only alternative would seem to be some form of monitoring of local decisions by central departments which would involve new and undesirable precedents in central control.

A description of institutional change tends to concentrate on formal aspects because these are the easiest to chronicle. Yet informal arrangements can be of great importance. The professional comradeship of senior officials helped to carry matters along. There were compacts not to appoint staff from a particular local authority department which was already under severe strain because other staff had left already. One hears of agency schemes that worked in practice, but which were never formally signed, because the authorities concerned were unable to agree on points of detail. Some authorities due to be joined together had an understanding about a target for cash balances to be held on takeover day; such understandings could not be other than informal as there was no possible means of enforcement. Another category of informal decisions related to the distribution of jobs. Members of councils being joined together might agree on some 'fair' distribution of senior posts on the new authority between the chief officers of the expiring units.

Whether local government gained benefit from the large turnover in senior personnel is a matter for argument. Certainly much ability and experience was lost through the early retirement of senior staff. As a result younger people gained unexpected promotion. Officers in unfamiliar roles and unfamiliar places had to face problems that they had not met before. Less movement of staff would have meant less need to learn about local situations. On the other hand, it may be said that new measures need new men; that the stimulus gained from promotion and movement should outweigh the disadvantage of loss of experience.

The strains of reorganisation made local authorities ever more dependent on the goodwill of their staff. This was recognised at the outset by the efforts made to keep staff informed about the coming changes and to dispel fears about redundancy and disturbance. Inevitably the anxiety lasted a long time; there was a long wait from when changes became certain to when the new authorities fixed their establishments and made appointments. Reorganisation increased the importance of NALGO as the union was successful in protecting the interests of its membership. Before 1972 some local authorities tended to treat their office staff and their union in a mildly paternal fashion; subsequently such behaviour became impossible. Of course, the rising strength of NALGO was not solely due to reorganisation because the early nineteen-seventies was a period of general increase in trade union activity and militancy.

The foregoing chapters have shown the importance of the part played by the central government in steering the process of local change. As a result the new generation of chief officers may be more conditioned to the acceptance of central guidance than their predecessors. In future the civil service may also find it rather easier to watch over local affairs as there are so many fewer local councils. On the other hand, the new authorities are larger and stronger. The elimination of small units must mean that the average quality of their senior staff is much higher. Few authorities (excluding the third-tier) are now smaller in size than a parliamentary constituency, so each council can bring stronger pressure on one or more MPs to lobby ministers on its behalf. But the broad tendencies which favour uniformity and the integration of policies among public bodies are unaffected by the 1972 Act. In this context reorganisation may make little impact on the general direction of central-local relationships.

New institutions reflect the aspirations and shortcomings of the age which creates them. Thus the new forms of local government demonstrate the contemporary and sometimes conflicting desires to modernise, to equalise, to end anomalies and to make public business more democratic and efficient. If the outcome be disappointment, this is parallel to experience in other aspects of national life. The absence of a decision on finance illustrates the wider determination to avoid awkward choices. The tendency to ignore traits in human behaviour which run contrary to current nostrums is illustrated by the inattention to the deficiencies of large units—for example, the weakened sense of personal responsibility and motivation in big organisations. *The Times*'s first leader of 1 April 1974 argued that the theories that produced the changes were already out of fashion. 'It is unlucky that the reform comes into effect at a time when the received ideas that initiated it have passed into some disfavour.' The article concluded that the glamour of bigness had faded: the new enthusiasm was for specialised pressure groups which would be urging their claims on the new authorities in an unfavourable economic climate.

Larger organisations tend to be more rigid and to operate more strictly to a pattern of rules. This is not necessarily a matter for criticism. It is fairer to apply rules consistently than to make *ad hoc* decisions. Admittedly, equitable administration may have an adverse affect on those who had received favourable treatment. One county borough had given free bus passes to schoolchildren who lived just inside the statutory limits: these were withdrawn soon after the borough was absorbed into the county. Another important issue is how far the remoteness caused by large units was overcome by the measures of decentralisation. This question was outside the scope of my research which centred on problems of administration, not on the reactions of the public. But the effect of the remoteness of larger local authorities is felt not only by ordinary people. An MP representing a former county borough commented: 'From my point of view the reorganisation was a disaster. In the old days, when I had a problem, I would ring up the Civic Centre and talk to someone I knew and say, "George or Bill, will you sort this one out for me?" Now I don't know the chap on the other end of the phone and if I did he would not want to do business in this way.'

There is much vital research to be done on the new system of local government. A number of major investigations are required. How is corporate management working in practice? How do larger units of administration affect individual services and also the public? What is the effect of dividing the planning function between counties and districts? In the former county boroughs what have been the consequences of splitting responsibility for housing and the social services?

The other area which requires more thought and more action is local government finance. It is arguable that the whole success of the reorganisation is in jeopardy because it gave local authorities no fresh source of revenue. This rating system is already under heavy criticism as a regressive form of taxation. The heavy cost of reorganisation combined with inflation placed a strain on it that was politically unacceptable. The result has been higher and higher levels of central financial aid and the appointment of the Layfield Committee to review the whole field of local finance. Local government cannot be a vigorous, proud, independent system if each year it has to take a begging bowl to Whitehall to ask for more grant aid. The lack of attention given to finance is the most unsatisfactory feature of the 1972 Act. Until further action is taken to allow local authorities some more independent income the reorganisation of local government remains unfinished business. The alternative is for local government to fade fairly soon into mere local administration of centrally designed services.

NOTES

1. Para. 576 (iv); 1968–9, Cmnd 4040, xxxviii.
2. 1967, HMSO, para. 286.
3. 1970–1, Cmnd 4584, paras 5–9.
4. 1970–1, Cmnd 4506, para. 2.
5. 1970–1, Cmnd 4741.
6. See pp. 42–3 *supra*.
7. In the final flurry some vital material failed to appear until after the change-over date. The Compensation Regulations (SI 463 of 1974) were laid before Parliament on 21 March, came into operation on 29 March but were not issued by the Stationery Office until 5 April. DOE Circular 50/74 which explained the Regulations was dated 3 April. In fact, the delay was not serious because the content of the Regulations had been widely canvassed long before publication.

GENERAL INDEX

accommodation 27, 39, 40, 47, 50, 53, 101, 166
acquisition of 39, 60, 188
agency and 37, 80
contracts and 89, 90
location of 48, 52, 63–4, 86, 88, 131
shared by county and district 77, 84
transfer of 69–70, 71, 72
accounting systems 65
administrative headquarters, location of 26, 39, 48, 50, 52, 130, 131
administrative methods, harmonisation of 39, 50, 63–8, 99–100, 125
Advertisements (Hire Purchase) Act 1967 96
aerodromes see airports
agency arrangements 23, 37–8, 40, 51, 61, 77, 78–84, 136, 144, 145, 188, 191
Circular 131/72 81–3, 96, 108–9, 122
consumer protection 82, 84, 96
disputes 57, 80, 82–4, 96, 104, 105, 105n.6, 106, 109–10
highways 82, 84, 87, 102–6, 129
libraries, 82, 84, 108–10
planning 82, 84
property and 72
refuse disposal 82, 84, 122–3, 129
airports 22, 38, 70, 73–4, 91–2, 141
aldermen 12n.3, 53, 189, 190
Alexander, William P., baron 176, 178
allotments 22
Arbitration Act 1950 73
architects 35, 89–90, 179, see also chief officers
area committees 38, 85, 87, 100–1

area organisation 36–7, 84–8, see also decentralisation
area secretaries 85, 86
areas 11–20, 61, see also population
armorial bearings 41
art galleries see museums and art galleries
Association of County Councils (ACC) 172–8 passim
Association of County Secretaries 179
Association of District Councils (ADC) 172–3, 174
Association of Education Committees (AEC) 167, 169, 175–8
Association of Metropolitan Authorities (AMA) 171–8 passim
Association of Municipal Corporations (AMC) 29, 80, 82, 167, 168n.1, 169–73 passim, 176, 176n.5
associations of local authorities 28–9, 41, 42, 43, 61, 68, 81, 82, 139–40, 167–78, 184
central government and 168–9, 170, 177, 179
functions of 167–9
liaison between 174–5, 176, 177, 178
unification attempts 167–75
see also under names of individual associations
Attorney General v. de Winton 156
audit:
District 39, 65
internal 65, 103, 156
professional 39, 65

Bains report 20, 27, 28–45, 57, 59n.4, 63, 95n.1, 145, 175–6, 177, 184,

INDEX OF LOCAL AUTHORITIES
AND JOINT COMMITTEES